FROM A LIL "P" TO A CAPITAL

BASED ON A TRUE STORY

Email: lynda@actiontakerspublishing.com

Website: www.actiontakerspublishing.com

ISBN # (paperback) 978-1-956665-70-3

ISBN # (Kindle) 978-1-956665-67-3

Published by Action Takers Publishing™

Dedication

Also dedicated in loving memory to my Auntie Millie, Mildred Flowers.

Table of Contents

"Don't watch me; watch the moves I make"
~"Big Percy" Damien Lamar Roderick

Foreword

Snoop Dogg and me (circa 2001)

From a Lil "P" to a CAPITAL "P," by Big Percy, born Damien Lamar Roderick, is a book for amateur artists who are committed to fully expressing their talent in the world. It's a book that will help you understand the importance and necessity of many things you need to do:

- Remember where you came from, your family roots, and the environment in which you grew up

- Treat all people the same: set aside prejudice, stereotypes

- Value all connections, contribute with love, and the love comes back

- Keep yourself safe and out of jail; once you're in, it's *hard* to get out. If you're in prison, it's probably too late

- See your truest, natural and authentic skills and aptitude; develop that as your path to your greatest success

- Success only follows when you are in harmony with your truest self. The world waits on you being *You*

Big Percy approached this book with the young, up-and-coming artist in mind. As a witness to the content in this writing, I can tell you wholeheartedly, it's a *powerful* read for Anyone. Dive in! And as Percy would say, "Don't watch me; watch the moves I make."

Helena Hope Wall

Co-Writer of this book, From a Lil "P" to a CAPITAL "P"

CHAPTER 1

A Real Pomona Love Story

"Big P! Percy is an absolute go-getter. No other way to put it. We go back to house party game nights before we all had kids and became full-fledged grown ups. That man has always had one foot forward. From OG to CEO, seemingly overnight. Everyone that knows him, rocks with him. And that's saying a lot in this industry. God Bless you P! Onward and upward. When you run for President, you'll have my vote!"
~Omar Gooding

Omar Gooding and me (circa 2017)

Introduction: A Life Like a Movie

I've been told numerous times that my life is like a movie. I've also been told I should write my story. I've heard it, and I've thought about it, now here it is!

My government name is Damien Lamar Roderick, but people have called me "Big Percy" or "Big P," "Uncle P" or just "P," for something close to 30 years.

Roots in Pomona

My first true love that I want to tell you about is my home city of Pomona. After all the places I've traveled and now live, Pomona is where everything started for me. My heart and soul always know, Pomona is home.

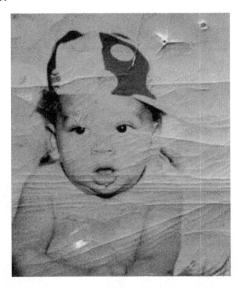

I was born in the city of Upland, which is two cities away from Pomona, but then my parents brought me home to my first home, in the city of Pomona.

Pomona is one of the last cities in LA County. We've always had to fight for ours and hold our own identity because of the distance that we are from the heart of Los Angeles, which is South Central. We always got a lot of flack from both sides, LA County and the I.E. (Inland Empire). From street life, to music life, to entertainment life, we've had to come a little harder, come a little tougher, because a lot of people didn't consider us LA County. The LA County Fair has been in our city for 100 years. That should tell you everything.

San Bernardino and the IE were viewed as being a little bit slower and a little bit behind the times. I've lived in both. I went to school in both. I've had family in both. So I've always had to play both sides of the fence.

Younger me

Growing up in Pomona, living in Pomona, was a great place, *is* a great place. In my younger days, of course, you were able to move around regardless of what section and what part of Pomona you lived in. Everybody went to the same YMCA, the same boys club, and the same swimming pool. And it was a good time because I had family in different sections and different parts of Pomona, regardless of the gang element. It was more family oriented in the '70s.

Adapting to Change

As times changed, the gangs and the hustling and all the different factors migrated from different parts of Pomona and it got a little bit worse. Many of my family members stayed in Pomona. My parents didn't want my brother and me to get caught up in a lot of that. So we moved to the next city, Ontario, which happens to fall in the Inland Empire in San Bernardino County. It was an up-and-coming area, growing, and it was a little bit nicer. It didn't have all the different factors and gang elements that were coming into Pomona.

I did a little bit of elementary school and a little bit of junior high in the city of Ontario. Then once that city got bad, my parents packed up and moved us to the next nicest, newest city, which was the city of Rancho Cucamonga. This is smack dab in the middle of the IE in San Bernardino County. I did pretty much all of my high school years in Rancho Cucamonga.

It's an evolution, a revolution of times and how things change. My mom and dad didn't want us to get caught up in the different elements and the different factors. I was privileged to be able to move so I wouldn't get caught up in it. It was definitely a blessing because of course you have two young men, my brother and I, with ethnic backgrounds and my parents were looking out for our well-being.

They wanted to move up to bigger and better homes, better schools and everything. It was a huge blessing. And it played a major factor in my life; it made me a better, well-rounded person because I had to adjust. I had to adapt to the different races that were around me. During my early youth, Pomona was predominantly Black and Hispanic. Then we moved to Ontario and it's predominantly White and Hispanic. And then, Rancho Cucamonga, which is predominantly White.

So it was just a change in the times, better opportunities, better schools, a little bit safer. And then that's why I say I don't have any problems with the IE because I lived there, was educated there, and was able to see the transformation of the different cities in my youth, which (all these cities are border cities) Ontario borders Pomona and Rancho Cucamonga.

I've actually seen everything from LA County and everything from IE from my adolescence to my adult life. I was able to factor those lessons into my lifestyle, and into my business. I am able to adapt anywhere and am able to move around anywhere and fit in. That's a very, very big privilege. Most people don't have that privilege. Most people are just stuck in their environment. And that's just another facet of me being able to share my experiences and give back. People see how well cultured and diverse I am because of it.

My primary residence now, though, is in Las Vegas and different parts of California, but still in LA County. I don't actually lay my head in the city of Pomona, but my kids know where I'm from. They know where their grandmother's from, and a lot of their cousins. My two kids visit Pomona. I took the same approach that my parents did. I wanted my kids to grow up in a nicer, better opportunity, better school district. So my kids are "in the suburbs of LA County and the suburbs of the Inland Empire." That's just based off the way I was raised, providing and giving my kids a better opportunity; to live in a more peaceful and conducive environment for them to grow and succeed.

That's what I'm trying to do. Provide a peaceful and conducive environment for them to grow and succeed. It's the foundation for the legacy, to create for my children and for the younger-than-me artists that I deal with. I want to let them know that, of course, we all come from where we come from. However, the bigger picture is, don't ever forget where you're from. The end goal is to get out of that environment and to see other things and grow.

That should be everybody's end goal; everyone who's in the street life, in the music life and the entertainment life. We all come from humble beginnings and poverty-stricken areas, but you don't have to stay there. There is more for you. And once you become more productive and more successful than whatever you're doing, the end goal is to get out of that environment and have your family in a better situation. I feel it's an opportunity for anybody and everybody.

That is 100 percent my message. There's no limitations on what you can do, no limitations on where you can live, no limitations on where you can go to school. It's all about the outlook and the energy and the environment that you want to be a part of.

Some people don't want to leave the hood and I get it, because that's where they're comfortable. But if you're trying to expand and grow and build and have better, sometimes the hood is not conducive to what you're trying to do and accomplish. The first step for people who want to progress may be to open their mind to changing that environment and then seeking the ways to do that.

I've always done it. Any time I've had an opportunity to take some of my younger cousins to get out of the neighborhood and go to other places, other countries, and other cities on tour with me or go to different events in Beverly Hills or Calabasas or Newport Beach, or taking them on the road, I always did that because I want them to see how big and beautiful the world is, and how many opportunities are out there. It's unlimited once you open up and knock down those barriers and walls.

My book and my message is about a real Pomona love story from my city. It's just everything to me. It's where I went to school, where I developed my hustle, where I developed my game and where my grandmother migrated and gave everybody in our family an opportunity. And as jobs and different things came into the city of Pomona, my family was at the forefront. It was the place where my dad went to college out of the army. It was the place where my dad expanded his career in sports, and teaching and counseling. It's everything to me. Without the city of Pomona, there is no Big Percy. There is no Roderick Music Marketing (RMM). There's nothing. So it is a real, real love story for me. Everybody knows that wherever I go, I'm pushing my city.

Sugar Shane Mosley is a boxing legend who comes out of the city of Pomona. He's a boxing champion, and he's known for community activism. His father was a boxing trainer and coach for him. But he's a legend out of our city, so it always gave kids like me and other kids, even though we didn't box, the idea that we could make it. Just seeing somebody who made it out of our city was enough. One of the first premier athletes that I can remember and still have a relationship with to this day, is Sugar Shane Mosley.

The Impact of Sports

Just like the city of Pomona was my foundation, sports was my avenue for not getting fully entrenched into the gang life because the OGs, the double OGs and the triple OGs and the gangsters in my neighborhood, and even the gangsters and the people that were active in my family knew that I had something more in me, other than the street life. They tried to persuade me not to get involved, even though I was pulled in and was intrigued by the street life and the hustle and the gang life.

They kept me away because they knew I had skills and talent that were bigger than that.

That skill happened to be basketball. Even though I was always playing basketball, my first real everyday love and everyday sport was soccer. I played club and indoor soccer. I played every level of soccer. I look back at it now as a blessing because there are not too many African-American kids playing soccer.

I was able to get into a sport that was mixed. It was predominantly Whites and Latinos, and I was able to mingle and carry my own. I was great at soccer. I was probably one of the top soccer players in my age division coming up. As I got taller, my love for basketball was natural. I would have played soccer in high school, but soccer and basketball were at the same time. So I had to make a choice. At that time, looking at a way out and looking at the economical side of sports, there was no money in soccer at that time. Looking at it as a business and a career move or getting a scholarship, basketball just made more sense for me. I had to choose.

Team photo shoot / high school basketball (circa 1989)

Basketball Dreams and Challenges

I was an all around natural athlete. All the coaches from all the sports wanted me to play football. I wasn't playing football because I didn't want to get hit, but I got into track and field because I was a great athlete. I was running and doing all the long jumps, breaking records. It was during one of my physicals that it was discovered I had a small heart murmur. That kind of scared me and my family. I pulled away from track and got the heart murmur taken care of. We nipped it in the bud.

Then as basketball grew, it became a year-round sport for me. I really had no time for anything else but full-time basketball. I was one of the top high school players all four years in my area and went to one of the most prestigious high schools in Southern California. I made my name and my claim to fame in high school basketball. From there, I had numerous scholarship offers, but I took the junior college route because of my dad's status; it was where he coached and taught, and it was a family tradition. So I took the junior college route and played for one year.

Celebrity basketball game/slam dunk contest UNLV early '90s

Then I transferred to the University of the Pacific up in Stockton, another prestigious college. I transferred there because one of my old high school teammates went there and established himself at the same institution, and he had a great career. I wanted to follow in his footsteps. I had numerous other offers, but it went back to some of the things I was doing in my life and I needed to get away from Southern California and try something new.

I went up to Northern California and took a three-year scholarship. There were some things that I didn't want to follow me into school and I needed a fresh start. So I went up north, played there for a year and I ended up only playing three games. I was getting homesick and had a falling out with my girlfriend at the time. I was going through a lot of different things mentally that I wasn't prepared for.

A Turning Point: From Courts to the Streets

Finally, I took a big leap and the next big step. I stepped away and got offered to go overseas and play some overseas basketball and make some good, lucrative money. I signed a six-month contract to play in the Philippines, and another six-month contract to play in Istanbul, Turkey. When I came home on a visit, I got into some trouble and kind of ruined everything for going back to my pro contract.

From there I had another opportunity to continue my basketball career. My choices were to either go pro with the NBA or go back overseas. Magic Johnson (Earvin "Magic" Johnson Jr.) took a liking to me and I played on his travel all-star team for about two months, traveling with him, playing in different invitationals and tournaments and showcases. I had one foot in basketball, and one foot in the streets.

Me with Snoop Dogg and Magic Johnson (circa 2020)

Dad with Magic Johnson (circa 2023)

At this time, I'm about 25. I left college, and went pro overseas. Magic gave me that opportunity to fulfill some goals. But, I had one foot in, one foot out. We had to sit down and talk; he could tell that I wasn't focused, and this wasn't what I wanted to do. That's when I ended up getting caught up in some major trouble and went to jail.

I was facing 25 years to life in prison. I was exonerated, cleared of all charges. I didn't make it to prison, by the grace of God, but I risked going away for a very long time. I was in jail, fighting my cases for over a year and a half. Prison is your last stop; that's when it's over. You get sentenced and there's no coming back. Jail is where you're fighting your case, doing all your preliminary hearings, your pre-trials and everything else. And you still have action on the streets and hopes of becoming free.

So I've never been to prison in my life. I've been to jail several times on dumb stuff as a youth, disorderly conduct, and fighting some other small cases and charges. But this particular one, I was facing some serious time, 25 years to life, in prison. With the wisdom that I'd had, from going overseas, the blessings of my family and my dad putting up his house and putting up some money, I was able to acquire Johnny Cochran's law firm.

At the time that Tupac, and OJ, and Mike Tyson were fighting their cases, I was fighting mine. Johnny Cochran's law firm used their resources to fight and it worked out in my favor.

The Birth of a Hustler

After my jail time, it was no more basketball or pro sports; it was over. I was a little bit older. I was traumatized and shell-shocked. It was time to get in and really try to make some money and figure out my life. And yeah, I was done with basketball as far as playing.

After that, I jumped full-fledged into the music game. The beginnings of my company, 100 percent started right when I got out of jail. And it was time to get into hustle mode and figure out what was next. Around this time, my cousin had a record label. I knew so many different artists from the city of Pomona and other cities. And I was pretty much already doing management-quality-type things for these artists. And it just came to the forefront with my cousin having a record label.

> *"Why don't I just become a real full-time manager and help these artists; help them to the next level with my connections and my know-how?"*

And from there it grew. I built so many different relationships. One of the artists from the city of Pomona, which is now my brother, was Kokane. He is one of the founders and the forefathers of Hip Hop and rap music in our city. Kokane was working with Warren G and The Dogg Pound and Snoop for years before I even thought of getting into the music business. I was a fan and Kokane started bringing me around and I started managing him. From there, Kokane introduced me to Snoop.

This was my first time at The Dogg House

This was my first real day with Dogg

These connections that I had, 90 percent came from the world of sports. That's where I made my name. I played on some of the top basketball teams and played with some of the top players that made it to the NBA. My name really was ringing bells from basketball. And my name was ringing bells from my cousin's record label; what he was doing and making noise.

I was always a people person and a hustler and had my hands in a lot of different things. A hustler is somebody who finds a way to make cash out of nothing. It's a way of putting plays together that weren't even there. It's connecting people. It's bringing this entity with that entity to make a bigger entity. It's connecting this person that never had a relationship or opportunity, to deal with that person. And you put that together and now you're a part of that business and you're basically quarterbacking a lot of different deals just off your gift of vocab, being able to adapt, being able to go to different cities, being able to sit down with different people.

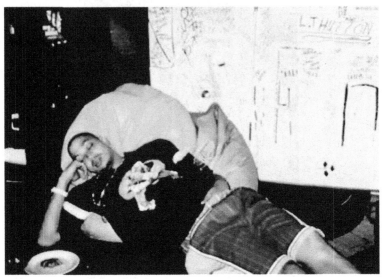

Long days and nights at the original Doggy Style Studios (circa 1999)

That's what a hustler is. And relating with people so that they all want to talk with you. Most people don't know how to talk to different races. Most people don't know how to connect the dots based on people's egos, and I never had that problem. My family was always making moves to improve my opportunities and it was the prime foundation for me, 100 percent.

I was very fortunate, but I was also very fortunate to see what was going on, seeing the opportunities, seeing that there was more for me other than this street life and the bullshit that was around.

I was able to implement that throughout the years. And now I'm doing the same thing with implementing it into how I raise my kids and implementing how I handle and run my business. The ability to take whatever the situation was, improving on it and also monetizing it was

100 percent natural. Not everybody can do it. Some people have talent, and some people have business sense, but many people don't know how to capitalize and put their talent and business into play for the greater good and become successful.

The key is, and people don't want to say it because they don't want to seem too greedy or egotistical is this: the end result is making money and generating a profit. The end result is creating something and getting something of value out of it. So, I've seen so many different opportunities that were lacking around a lot of artists and talent. And I thought, "You know what? This is my opportunity to step in and bring these business deals and opportunities to these artists. Opportunities they didn't even know were sitting out there."

That's a major, major talent to have. And it goes back to being able to move around freely, speak to anybody, not showing any prejudice, not showing any bias, and not looking at it through color.

It has always been my gift that I've had. It was fostered by the upbringing that I had and my parents' efforts to always improve things for me. I can't speak for somebody that hasn't had the same opportunities that I have had. I know I've been blessed.

I've also had to face ridicule and backlash because a lot of people in my neighborhood, in my city, say I was privileged. Of course I *was* privileged a little bit more than others, because I had both parents in the house. Both my parents had good jobs. I'm not going to say I took advantage of that. I was just blessed. So I had to hear from the streets and homies and other cousins, "Oh, he's spoiled. He got this because of this and that." No, I *worked* for it. My parents *worked* for it. My family *worked* for it.

I wasn't immune to the ridicule even though I had privileges. It wasn't the only thing that was there for me. I still had to work. I still had to put my talent, my God-given abilities; I had to put them into fruition. I had to put them into action because talk is cheap. And a lot of people can talk, but can you walk it?

That's just another thing that I've always had in me. If I say I'm going to do it, I'm going to do it; what I say goes. And that thinking has carried on into my business world as well.

Somebody who doesn't have the same talents, what can they do?

"Everybody has something that they can offer."

So just figure it out, find out what your *something* is, your *'it factor'* and go out there and do *that*. That's exactly what we did when we took these kids from the Long Beach City Movement and the Pomona City Movement on their first tour. We gave them an opportunity to see the world and they got paid for every show.

Long Beach City Movement (circa 2002)

Pomona City Movement (circa 2017)

Pomona City Movement (circa 2017)

These kids were doing shows and doing music for years and they never were able to expand it and see some kind of residual income or payment for what they were doing until Snoop and I gave these kids opportunities. But like everybody knows, I don't sugarcoat shit. If your music sucks, I'm going to tell you, that's why you're coming to me. Because you want honesty.

I always tell these guys, you might not be the artist that's going to be on the stage. You might be a better manager. You might be a better producer. You might be a better person that knows how to work these cameras, or a booking agent. It's just based off what I see in you and I'm going to tell it to you real so you can take that direction and figure it out on your own. I don't want you wasting your time on something that's not going to be beneficial for you later.

I don't sugarcoat it. If your music is just regional music for your neighborhood and your friends, I'm going to tell you that. If your music is international, worldwide, and I see something in you, I'm going to put you in those right positions. But if I see you making moves and connecting dots and bringing people together, I'm going to tell you, "you know what, you might be a promoter and you might be a better manager because you're bringing all this talent around and they're coming; it's coming from you. You got a gift in *that*."

To hone in on the right field is important. Somebody could be feeding them this line that, "I know it's in you. I know it's in you," till the cows come home, yet it never happens. In the end, what has that done for that person? It can destroy their life by giving false hope and leading them down the wrong path.

Well, that's 99% of the entertainment and music world. It's all lies and smoke and mirrors. Not too many people are truthful because the people that are telling them this bullshit are really looking out for themselves.

What can they gain and what can they take for themselves? A lot of these so-called managers and promoters and agents are taking these kids' ideas, taking these kids' money, and other things. And it's ruining them. It's really ruined the opportunities that they could have had if they would have told them the truth.

Building a Legacy

Entrepreneurship, for me, just came from many, many years of working with Snoop and seeing the different trials, tribulations, struggles and losses that he had, things like not getting paid for his work, not getting the lion's share of the proceeds because managers, promoters, corporate Americans were using him and taking advantage of him. I saw it. I've seen it from Snoop, which being on the top of the food chain, the icon, the middle artist, the lower level artists, I've seen it so much. And it just came to a point that I didn't want to be like that. And I wanted to be a tastemaker and a real culture icon.

I wanted to build and have some things for myself because I've seen what corporate America was doing to my friends. And so that's when it came to the point of saying, okay, we're making these liquor companies all this fucking money and they're giving us crumbs. Why don't we start our own liquor company? If these clothing companies are giving us free clothes to wear on the road and promote for them. Why don't we make our own clothes? We are shopping at all of these different stores that are charging us high fees. Why don't we open our own stores?

Empowering the Culture

It came to the point that *we are the culture.* We are the tastemakers. We are everything to these businesses and companies. Let's just start making our own products and our own merchandise.

This 100% laid the groundwork for beginning to work with Snoop Dogg as his manager. He had so many different managers and so many people chomping at him and lying to him and stealing from him and promising him stuff. I was studying and I was observing and I instantly, when I first came around him, I brought him X amount of dollars for this, X amount of dollars for that, and brought this to the studio and brought this to the team and came up with so many different things that they didn't have access to or people were denying them or people were not exposing them to all these different opportunities.

I was bringing it to him naturally because I'm around him. One, I was a fan and I was just happy to be around some of my idols in the music business. And I had access to just be around him. And I knew there were so many different opportunities.

Once people started finding out that I was working with him and always around him, so many people would approach me with different opportunities. And then I would bring it to him or The Dogg Pound or Warren G or all the different facets that were in our camp. From there, we were seeing the fruits of our labor. The money was just flowing. That was like my niche around Snoop. Everybody knew "P" was a hustler. Everybody knew "P" was going to make an opportunity. Everybody knew if we needed to get some money or needed some great ideas, "P" was the man.

Doggy Style Records (circa 2000)

Player's Ball Tour Life (circa 2000)

CHAPTER 2
Mom and Dad

"Big Percy is a true Go-Getter. Ever since I've known him, he's been a mover and a shaker. Always keeping his hand on the pulse of what's happening in the world, what's happening in the streets, what's happening in business. He never lets himself get caught in any one particular bag. That's one thing I like about him. He's a guy that's driven to make things happen, from his liquor brands to moving concerts around, being plugged in with some of the top, top people in his business. He is a connector, using his powers and resources to make things happen for himself and for others, and that's an important skill set. When you know how to move the meter for yourself, that's one thing. When you know how to move the meter for others, then you are a useful individual, and that's what Big P always learned, knew how to do, how to make himself necessary and needed in the situation. It's part of the leader of the Rider Gang, our car club. He is one. He put it together, started out with four cars. Before you knew it, we had hundreds of cars riding out on the streets of Los Angeles as a businessman and entrepreneur for many businesses. True legacy. His vodka brand is great, doing big stuff. Always a plug. Shout out to Big P. Go get 'em, Roderick."
~Ced the Entertainer

The Beginning of a Love Story

The story of my mom and dad started when my grandmother was the head cook at California State Polytechnic University, Pomona ("Cal Poly Pomona"), in the city of Pomona, and my dad was a football star at that college.

Dad at Cal Poly Pomona

My Auntie Mildred was dating a guy on the football team, and of course my mom would follow wherever her big sister went. My grandmother already knew my dad because he was a football star and a starving student, and she used to go out of her way to feed some of the guys extra; sometimes when they didn't have money or whatever the case would be, she would sneak the guys into the cafeteria and feed them.

Like I said, my aunt was already dating somebody on the team and knew players, and that's how my mom and dad began hanging out—through her. Then once it came to them dating, of course you have to go to see grandma. Since Grandma already knew my dad, they started dating and developed a relationship.

My dad, who's a little older, played football in college and had aspirations of playing in the pros. Eventually, they got married, and my grandmother helped my dad pay for my mom's ring.

Family portrait (circa 1980)

Family Roots and Early Memories

I am my parents. I'm my dad in so many ways, and I'm my mom in so many ways, but in my youth, we were a close family. All I knew was my mom and my dad and having them both providing for me and them both being there was a blessing. There was a lot of love in the house. I would say, throughout the years, you have your trials and tribulations and, you go through your different things. You could step away from this family member or that family member or that friend or whoever, for whatever reason. I've done that with both parents throughout my 51 years, but I would say I'm equally close to both of them. They still support me. They both come to my events. When I have events that they can enjoy, like my golf tournament or birthday events or kids' events, or other family members' events, birthdays, graduations or whatever, they both show up and they're generous and everything else.

My mom is a lot like my grandmother. She is the baby of her siblings; I'm the baby of my family.

My mom (circa 2014)

My mom (circa 2017)

My dad (circa 2023)

Dad at my golf tournament (circa 2021)

A Family Transition

I was between 7 and 10 when my mom and dad divorced. My dad didn't want a crazy transition from me, so he helped my mom get a condo right down the street from our big house. So I was able to go back and forth on my own, whether it was walking or riding my bike. But it was just an easy transition so that I would see both of them and spend equal time with both of them in the same neighborhood. So I had that dynamic, until probably sixth grade.

Then my mom got involved with another guy. And they lived together all the way up until my junior high years. Then from there, my mom moved and got her own place. And that was pretty much all my high school years. During high school, she probably was dating, but there was nobody living in the house with me and her. Since divorcing my dad, she lived with two other people that I know of. Has she dated other people? Yeah. But if it wasn't a serious situation, I didn't have a relationship with them.

The Power of Co-Parenting

My parents kept a friendship and were cordial because of the kids. Then later, I would say growing to be very tolerant of each other and respectful of each other's situation. My parents did a great job of co-parenting and making sure time was spent at both homes. I wasn't able to play both sides of the fence because they had communication.

The Bond Between Brothers

My brother is five years older. We had a great relationship as kids. Everybody knew it was Gaynell and her two boys. Mom kept us together through everything. Even though my father wasn't my brother's biological father, if I went, he went. If I did, he did. So he was always with me. That's something that they kept together. It was their plan to keep us together. And they did a great job of it. So if I went to my dad's, my brother came. If I went and did some stuff, if I went somewhere, my brother went. We had the same mother, but different fathers, but we were brothers.

Sports and Family Life

My mom was very self-sufficient, very family oriented, and supported us through all our endeavors. My mom was an athlete and so was my dad, which I think has a lot to do with their relationship. My dad actually at one time coached my mom's women's softball league. He also played softball and they played coed softball together. When my mom and dad were married, they were in bowling leagues together. When they separated, they stayed in softball and bowling leagues together. So seeing those things growing up and being around that stuff as a kid had a major influence on me and my brother's sports world, and sports life.

My mom and dad still call and text each other on birthdays. When my kids have something going on, they're both there. They joke around at my golf tournaments. They have a lot of interaction. My dad came to my grandmother's funeral and he said his words and came to the repass after, and spent time with us. Everybody in my family knows my dad because the junior college we went to. Most of the nephews and cousins went to that school at some point. And my dad was a part of their life at the school as well, just like he was with me.

I think my dad got involved with somebody else and got caught cheating. My mom found out and she wasn't having it. I don't know the fine intricate details, but as I got older, I saw things and figured things out on my own, I never saw any of the arguing and fighting, but I know my dad got caught cheating or was involved or was dating someone outside the marriage and he ended up marrying. And they are still married to this day.

My parents have a good relationship now, but it didn't happen overnight. My dad maintained a good relationship with my mom, probably for my sake. Especially since my dad was remarried and I was going back and forth to their house. That was probably his way to make peace.

My mom kept it apparent that that's how things were going to go regardless of what happened. She didn't take my dad away from me. She could have, but she didn't. That's something you don't see nowadays. Many women would set down all relationships with the kids and their father based on their own feelings. My mom didn't do that. She maintains a good friendship with the father of her kids. That doesn't happen in this era of parenting today. It doesn't happen. It's not the norm.

I don't often say anything negative about anybody in my family. I learned that from my grandmother, 100%. There's all types of different people and families and different dynamics and all that stuff. If they're, per se, on some bullshit or living a different lifestyle in a different way, instead of down-talking and down-playing and doing any of that, I just go my own way and choose not to be around it. But they're still family, I still have love for them. I just know how to separate myself, to not be into the drama and get in the middle of it.

And there's opportunities for them to come back around and prove themselves and all that stuff. But me, personally, I don't have time to deal with it. I've got other things. I've got my own problems, my own kids to worry about.

Lessons from Dad

Like I said, *I am my father, I am my mother.* So all my educational background, the books and how important that was supposed to be or how people portray it to be, I lived by structure, and discipline came from Dad. Mom was a little more lenient and let me get away with a few different things and hang out and do certain things. But my pop's military background, everything connected with that, I take that from him. He instilled that into me and I appreciate it a whole lot because without that structure and discipline, I definitely would have been into the other side of the street a lot faster.

My dad, even though he was educated and went to school and coached and did professor and counselor and all those things, he still is self-made; started coaching at the very lowest level, high school, worked his way up from high school to junior college, got his feet into junior college and never left. He established and opened up so many doors for himself, which opened so many doors for not just me being a student athlete, but so many student athletes across the world and successful pro athletes.

Dad's Influence Beyond Family

He opened those doors that still, to this day, I encounter so many people that my dad has helped and touched. Just off the top of my head, because his name is in the forefront, the Las Vegas Raiders' head football coach, Antonio Pierce, my dad was a major influence in that guy's life and they still have a great relationship and even a better relationship with Antonio's father. Antonio Pierce was one of the top football players in the city of Long Beach. My dad took a liking to him and got him to Mt. SAC to play football. And then from Mt. SAC, he got a scholarship to play at Arizona State, got drafted to the Giants, won a Super Bowl ring with the Giants, went on to coach, is doing coaching. I'm not going to say following in my dad's footsteps, but he went into coaching back at Long Beach Poly. From high school, he coached at the college level. From the college level, he coached in the pro level. Then when the opportunity came, after the Raiders fired their coach, he was on the coaching staff and the team loved him. The players loved him. The organization loved him so much. He never had a head coaching job in the pro level and they gave him the Raiders head coaching job. That's just one example.

And that guy has not strayed. He hasn't changed his way. He still drives his lowrider Impala to work every day because, like he said, it's his era, he was always a Raiders' fan because the Raiders were always the bad guys and the rebels. At the time he was growing up, NWA (it stands for 'niggas with attitude') was the big music. He still carries that mantra. They wore all the Raiders gear and that was kind of the Raiders' mantra. Now for him to be the Raiders' coach, it's a full circle moment.

My dad and Antonio's dad still come to support the Mt. SAC events and athletes. Antonio's dad actually came to a couple of my daughter's basketball games this year. Antonio has been honored several times up at Mt. SAC. My dad has honored his dad as well. These types of stories (I have hundreds of them) are off the top of my head.

Mom's Loudest Legacy

My mom, she didn't take to sports growing up, I don't even think she played sports in high school. When she became an adult, I think sports was something she and my dad bonded over. My mom was a great softball player and a decent bowler, and she connected with many friends through those activities, but she never took it any further than that. My mom's influence focused on her family, my brother and me, her nephew, my oldest cousin. She supported us all. She brings that same support to my daughter's basketball career. My mom goes to my daughter's games wherever they are. Anybody that played, whether it was me, my brothers, my cousins, or my daughter, she was at those games. My mother's claim to fame is that she was always the loudest person. She was the loudest! She cussed out the refs, she would cuss us out for messing up, so not on the cheerleader nice side, rah rah. She was the rowdy one if you did something wrong, coach, player, other team, other cheerleaders, she was on your ass.

My daughter, Isabella, college basketball game at Mt. SAC (circa 2023)

Unbreakable Family Support

My mom used to come to my games and you could hear her. I mean timeout, she yelled. The ref made a bad call, she yelled. When I take her to football games or bigger events now, she's the same way. She even yells at the TV.

Yeah, if you don't want her at the game, she'll tell you, "Don't invite me and don't tell me how to act." That's my mom in that aspect of sports. My mom was a big supporter of everybody in the family. She had a relationship with everybody in the family, adults, kids, whatever and she still is that way today.

CHAPTER 3

Grandma

---

*"Big Percy is an unbelievable Father, Friend, Mentor,
and Business Partner... a Workaholic who appreciates the
grind of working hard to provide for family and business
opportunities for associates.. life of the party and brightens
any room he's in with his Love and Fellowship!! 'Church on
the Move,' 'He Had To Do It.'"*
~O.J. Mayo, former NBA college star

O.J. Mayo (used with permission)

The Heart of the Family: Grandma's House

Grandma's house was the epicenter for everybody in the heart of the city of Pomona. It's the same house she moved to from San Francisco. She had gotten a little apartment. Then after the apartment, she purchased that home. We still own that home today. I actually have first action on buying it, and revamping it, and doing some stuff with it. It was left to her kids, my mom, my uncle, and my auntie. If I buy it, then I'm going to build one or two more houses in her backyard, just to supplement the income.

The main house that my grandmother lived in will be open and accessible for anybody in the family that needs a place to stay, or when they come into town to visit. We can keep her house in the family forever, because it just holds so many memories.

My grandmother hasn't even been gone a year, so it will be at least another year before I buy it. That's more time to honor her memory. It'll be in my living trust and stipulated in my will that nobody can sell it.

My goal and plan would be to let my oldest cousin, George Hardin, stay in the front house. George is the oldest grandkid, and he knows every in and out of that house, because he was always doing maintenance for my grandmother. He will be the caretaker. He is somebody that's been in that house since he was born, and anytime my grandmother needed some work, paint, whatever she needed, she called him first.

A Mentor and a Lesson in Redemption

George's nickname is Andre or Dre. Since he is the oldest grandson, and being a basketball star, it paved a way for me to follow in his footsteps as far as basketball went. I also learned from some of his heartaches, his hardships and his mistakes so I can try to avoid them.

Sugar Bear, Andre, Uncle Milton and me (circa 2004)

But, living in those environments and being a hard-head knucklehead, I did fall into some of the same things that he had fallen into just because of where we grew up and the attraction to the street life. I *did*, but I was able to make my adjustment quicker and faster than he did. That all goes back to the opportunity that was open for me, that I didn't get into much *more* trouble.

Now, at his older age, I think he's seven or ten years older than me, he's got his life back on track, and hasn't been in any trouble. As a blessing, I was able to do something for him, and I know it made my family, especially my grandmother, my mom, and my auntie, very happy and very proud. I was able to pay off his parole and probation fees. He was able to get all the paperwork done so he could just be free.

My auntie lives around the corner from the house. When my mom comes into town, she stays at Grandma's house because they're still going through all her stuff. I think my uncle has stayed there one time since my grandmother's been gone. I've been over there once since she's been gone, but nobody lives there permanently.

Grandma's Selflessness and Final Wishes

That house was my grandmother's everything. She bought it on her own, paid it off on her own, rebuilt everything on her own. To my knowledge and to my remembering, she never had a man live there, and it was always, any time a family member called, needed a place to stay, needed to make a couple extra dollars, needed a meal, she opened that door for whoever was in her family at any time of the day. Until the day she died.

She did it completely by herself. Of course, in her older age, my auntie was her caregiver, but my grandmother was able to stay in her own home until her very last day. She wanted to die in her house, die in her own bed, and that's what we gave her, her wishes.

When she got sick and went to her last doctor appointment, they were trying to keep her there, but she told my auntie and my mom, "Take me home." They took her home, and she did all her peace. People came to see her and visit her, and then she got to go and pass at 92 years old in her bed just like she wanted.

A Full Circle Moment

My last visit with her was excellent. Her brain was sharp as a tack. She never lost her memory. Of course it deteriorated, but she never lost her memory. Her body shut down. I would always try to make my grandmother laugh. Even though she didn't look the same because she was losing weight, I have great memories of my last time with her. What made it a little easier for me was that my daughter started college and lived around the corner, and my daughter was in an apartment at the same college that my grandmother cooked at.

My daughter lived in those same apartments on that college campus, and my daughter drove herself in her own car like I used to do to visit my grandmother. My auntie and my grandmother cooked a meal, and my daughter sat on the same couch like I used to when I was in college. She did everything like I used to do. Same college, same everything, going and visiting my grandmother, visiting other family members, and that was a great highlight for me because it was just like my grandmother said, it was just like me being reincarnated.

I have pictures and all that stuff today, and one of the diamond necklaces that I have with my grandmother's face is from that day also.

Me wearing Granny's necklace

I made several pendants; that's one of them. And I try to wear one of the pendants every day with all my other jewelry, like my good luck charm now. I wear jade and other jewelry, but I always try to wear one of her pendants mixed in with all the other stuff.

Grandma's Treasures

My oldest daughter is still around the corner, she's just in transition, figuring out what she's going to do next year as far as athletics and job and everything. It's her second year of college. She's studying cinema; she's into cameras, photography, cinema, film, that's her major. She's been into cameras since she was a kid. She actually got to acquire some of my grandmother's old cameras.

Granny wasn't into cameras per se; she just had a collection of everything. She had cameras because when she traveled or whatever, she took pictures and used old camcorders, but I can't say that she was a photographer.

She did have a lot of photo albums and a lot of pictures, so it might have been one of her hobbies. All the stuff that she had camera-related we were able to pass it down to my daughter. My daughter got to go over to her house and pick out certain things. My mom, my auntie, and I let my daughter keep them. Just as well as they're doing for other family members, but it's a pecking order.

And guess what? All the gems, and all the prizes, and all the good stuff has not even been touched yet. There is a lot of that, hidden gems are in the garage, and we haven't even gotten to that part yet. We're just barely going through her room, one of the back rooms, and some of her closets. My daughter got to pick out a couple of nice leather jackets that my grandmother had. My little daughter just got a package with some stuff. My dad got some stuff from his old newspaper football clippings when he went to that college that my grandmother cooked at. My mom gave him some of those clippings. There was a lot of the stuff that I purchased for my grandmother throughout the years, and I got it back.

I have some in LA, and I have some in Las Vegas, and when I get back to Vegas, I will have a couple of different shrines. Some of the stuff that I gave her, I have to figure out where it all goes.

For my daughter's birthday this year, my grandmother had a stuffed animal that you push its ear or its foot it sings music, and I was able to bring it to my daughter's birthday. My little daughter loved it. Of course she wanted to keep it because it sang 'happy birthday to you,' and she knew it was from her great-grandmother. But I told her, "No, baby, I have to keep this one." She can play with it any time, but I had to keep this, and my grandmother had it brand new in a box, never taken out of the box. I think it was Barney the purple dinosaur. When you push its foot, it sings 50 songs.

Grandma's Wisdom Lives On

I'm sure I got *all* of my giving and helping people traits from my grandmother, because, even though she wasn't the richest, you would never know. She would always slide you $20. If my cousin needed some money, she'd make him come paint the gate, or take her trash cans out, and slide him a couple dollars.

I never really saw her upset. I barely, maybe once or twice, ever heard her say a cuss word. And she just stuck to her program, and never, ever wavered from it. Every family member who came into her house knew that no bullshit, no animosity, no hate was allowed once you passed the door. She didn't care if you had other problems with other family members. If the other family members were there, you better not stir up no bullshit at her house.

I remember those qualities of her, and I think I've taken a lot of those things, and incorporated them into my life. One of my special things that I always like to do, anytime I come into town, I would bring her lunch. When I was younger, she was able to eat different foods. In-N-Out and McDonald's were some of her go-tos. And then, of course, you gotta stop eating that stuff. So it's a famous little chicken place, with a hamburger stand, but it has so many different things. One of the things I would always get us, even if I could only stop there for 10 minutes, was a chicken plate. It came with chicken, french fries, salad, a rolled zucchini, and it would serve like four people. We would eat together, and she would be so happy because she was able to save some food, and freeze it, or chop it up in a salad for the next day. She knew she had dinner or lunch for two more days with the meal that I would bring.

In return, I knew I would leave with a Ding-Dong, or a couple apple juices, or soda, or whatever she had. She would always stack me up, and I would leave with something. When I was in college, I was a starving student. She would feed me, and give me all types of stuff, extra food, supplies, anything she thought I needed. She would buy things she knew that I liked, and when I would come over, she would tell me to take it home.

Pomona's Matriarch

I know our relationship was very, very unique, but I think in my neighborhood, and where I grew up, there were a lot of home-bases. In my neighborhood, it was usually Grandma's house, and the guys and kids I grew up with, my grandma was a key factor for a lot of those kids. The whole city of Pomona at that time, maybe a lot of the matriarchs, moved to Pomona for a better opportunity. Once those older people started having kids, that's where those kids stayed, and then they had kids, and raised their kids. I remember Pomona in my upbringing. There was a lot of structure and continuity coming from the grandparents' houses. That was like the hub for everybody. Somebody's grandparents lived in the neighborhood.

There's probably nobody in the city of Pomona that didn't know my grandmother, didn't know her grandkids. At one time, the mayor of Pomona's parents lived by my grandmother, and before she passed, my grandmother was the oldest living person who'd lived the longest in her neighborhood.

Granny *got to do it her way*. She had several opportunities to move where my uncle lived in Arizona, to move to Vegas when my auntie lived in Vegas, and a couple opportunities to buy some duplexes. The two females (my mom and auntie) could have shared a spot, and then my grandmother would have had a spot next door, but it never panned out because my grandmother was so content and happy and comfortable where she was. She had other opportunities to move, but she just did it her way, and everybody had to conform to her way and knew not to pressure her after she made her decision. So, yeah, 100% she did it her way. You just knew not to pressure her from where she was, and her kids fulfilled her last wish.

The first 50 years were pretty much how I laid it out. So just like my grandmother, I think about the next 50 years. They call me 'old blue eyes' for a reason, because just like Frank Sinatra said, *"I'm going to do it my way."*

My next 50 years will be pretty much what I'm feeling, what I'm doing, what I'm liking, where I'm living. I'm going to adjust and go with the flow of my vibrations on what I'm doing. If it's doing nothing and staying retired and staying out of the way, that's what I'm going to do. If I decide to jump into something else major, business-wise, I'm going to go full-fledged on that and make it successful.

It might just be traveling for the next 20 or 30 years until I hit that older age, because that's something I always wanted to do. If I had an opportunity or a trip, my grandmother just admired me doing it with no hesitation and *not waiting on anybody*. That was a blessing for me because I know she lived through me. She would always admire me traveling, going places with Snoop, being on the road or doing things, different opportunities that came my way. She always bragged about me doing stuff like that, and she didn't really have that opportunity because she had to work so much and provide for her family. It was a great blessing to call her from wherever I was and tell her where I was. Or, when I would call her, she would say, "Where are you at now?"

And then I'd just tell her where I was. I know she would be bragging to the other people in my family about how I would just go. So I've got a strong feeling that's how I'm going to continue.

She always prayed and worried and told me to watch who was around me and "everybody's not your friend." I would call her and let her know I made it or landed and told her where I was and what I was doing. I know she's still looking over me and concerned and worried and everything else because that's what she always did. Couldn't get away from that.

It's one of the best feelings in the world because I know I had a guardian angel when she was here, and I know I still have one with her being in the spirit world. She is the matriarch of everything that comes from my family and I. Now I think, without her, there's no me.

November 2024 was a year since my grandmother passed. But she's with me right now, talking to you. I have her on my necklace, that chain I made, and I wear it every day. I have murals all through my house, and all through my backyard. She's actually getting her mural put up as soon as the weather permits. She's getting a whole wall to herself. It's right by the pool, where I spend a lot of time, and it's right by my fire pit. She'll be able to look over the whole backyard and see me when I'm out there.

My grandmother made it to 92 years.

A Poignant Farewell

Both times my kids were born, that was the first place I took my daughters from the hospital, to see their great-grandmother, so grandma could touch them, love them, and spend her time with them. My grandmother had grand, great, and great-great grandchildren. She made it to that level. All of them knew her and spent time with her. All of them were touched and blessed by that woman. And my kids, especially because I spent so much time with my grandmother, I told them, "You got to come with me. You got to come get some of this wisdom. You got to see where I come from."

And when my little daughter was born, my grandmother had such a good relationship with both my ex-wife and my little daughter's mom. But the relationship that my little daughter's mom and her family had become so attached with my grandmother, my little daughter's mom wanted to name my little daughter after my grandmother. And my grandmother told her, "Do not do that to that little baby and give her my name," because my grandmother has an old southern country name. My grandmother's name is Lula Mae. And my grandmother told my daughter's mom, "Don't do that to that girl, she'll be teased her whole life having that name." So my daughter's nickname is Little Lula.

I'm Damien Lamar Roderick and my daughter is Destiny Love Roderick. So Destiny's and my initials are DLR. Her other name is Little D or Little DLR. I was Big D before I was Big Percy. So I'm Big D and Big DLR.

My daughter, Destiny, 3 years old (circa 2019)

Left to right - Little Destiny & Little Percy

Destiny just turned eight. At my grandmother's funeral, she was only seven and she shocked everybody. She's my grandma. She's so caring, so giving, so loving. She's mixed with all types of stuff. She's just like me. We're having all the same attributes and the same opportunities. I didn't want to go up to the casket and look in and all that stuff. I wasn't ready for all that, so I didn't do it. So my mom and my auntie and my uncle gave everybody the opportunity if they wanted to go to the casket. Some cousins did. Some family did. Some family didn't.

And then everybody had the opportunity to speak and say what they wanted to say about Granny. And my little daughter said, "Dad, I want to go up there and talk for Granny Lula." I said, "What?" So I took her to the front. I sat in one of the front pews and handed her off to my dad at first. And then my dad walked her up there and handed her off to my uncle and my cousin.

She got up there and gave her own speech, her own sermon, on her own. My oldest daughter didn't do it. Older kids didn't do it. She went up there so poised and said what she wanted to say and was clear as day and didn't even break down. She might have broken down once she got back to her seat. After that, she went to the casket. She had written something or drew a picture and went up to the casket and put it in. She spent seven years of her life with my grandma. Any time she got, she spent time at granny's house.

Granny's house was kind of a meeting spot, an in-between spot. It was a safe house. If you needed to get a meal while you're passing through, that's what Granny's house was for. If you were fighting with your baby mama, your ex-wife, or whoever she was, your spouse, and you had to pick up your kids from Granny's house, you left that shit at the door. Come in, be respectful, and then do what you have to do once you leave. But you knew you couldn't have any bullshit going into Granny's house. She didn't care who you were. She wasn't playing favoritism. She loved everybody the same.

The New Matriarch

Auntie Millie is the new head of household, the new matriarch of the family. She was the caregiver for my grandmother and she's always been one step below Granny. She's the same as Granny, just a lot more stern and a lot tougher. My aunt is getting older and worn out. She had to change her life to take care of her mom. So she missed out on a lot of things.

A Tribute to Auntie Millie

Sadly, Auntie Millie passed from this world just as I was putting the finishing touches on my book. May she rest in peace.

Family photo (circa 2022)

CHAPTER 4

Brotherhood and Bonds

"Big Percy is the most loyal man I've ever known. His heart is bigger than what he portrays, but his philanthropic ideas and what he does to help the community goes well beyond. I've had an opportunity to coach with him, and coaching is a calling. We were able to help these young men without any type of recall to him. He helps behind the scenes more than anything else. He's kind of like a godfather in that sense.

"He has his hand in with a lot of people, helping them be positive and do good, not just giving them money or anything like that, but really helping them advance in their faith and life. He's always been a person that I can count on, to talk to about different situations. In business, he's connected by his personal life and his family. In fact, his love for basketball is what really keeps us going through and through.

"He loves his daughter, the vice president of his company, and his other daughter too. Again, he's a wonderful father, a good friend, and a very, very smart businessman. He has a lot of connections. He has a famous quote that he likes to say, 'Don't watch me; watch the moves I make.' Yes, I would say exactly that. You watch how he does what he does, and then

actions always speak louder than words. Where his heart is, you can absolutely see it. If you're around him, you will never go hungry. You will always be safe and you will always be supported. There's no doubt in my mind."

~ Keith Hollimon

Front Row - Me, RIP Coach Criss Freeman, Keith Hollimon (circa 2007)

Roots in Memphis: Grandma's Journey

My maternal grandmother comes from Memphis. She didn't want to be in the environment with racial things that were going on, and she didn't want to work those kinds of jobs and pick cotton. So she was always looking for a better way. Some job opportunities came about as the car industry and the industrial industry started popping up in Detroit. So when she went to Detroit, she already had my uncle and my aunt. They're older than my mom, and those two kids are from the same father. She met my grandpa in Detroit.

My grandfather was already married, already had kids with another lady, and my grandmother got pregnant. She put the ultimatum down on my grandfather. Whatever took place during that time, grandma wasn't having it, so she picked up her three kids and looked for a better way, better job opportunity, and took them to San Francisco.

She wasn't flying and probably took a train or bus all the way to San Francisco from Detroit. She got a better job and started working for what I think was the bus station or school district.

From Detroit to San Francisco: A Mother's Resolve

My grandfather was not in my mom's life, so obviously he wasn't in my life. In her 40s or early 50s, they reconnected. My grandfather had (including my mom) about 17 kids. All the other kids were with the same lady, and then my mom was the one with my grandmother. So those kids wanted to meet their sister and her kids because I think my mom is now the oldest living sibling out of all those kids.

My grandfather and my mom started building a relationship. So we went to Detroit and did a family reunion with them over 30 years ago. And I built that relationship, and my mom built the relationship. My grandfather and I hit it off, all my aunts and uncles hit it off. We all had a great time. I'm in communication with them now. I'm actually older than one of my uncles. My grandfather passed, so my mom made amends with her dad.

The Pomona Connection

My brother and I have the same mother. When my grandmother moved everybody to San Francisco, that's when my mom met my brother's father and they had my brother. My mom and my auntie were hanging around the 'wrong' people and my grandmother wasn't liking the direction. Those guys were hustlers and moneymakers and Grandma didn't like her girls around that. My auntie just had my oldest cousin, and my mom just had my brother, so Grandma wasn't having it, so she packed up everybody and moved them all to the city of Pomona for a better opportunity. And that's how we got our roots in the city of Pomona.

A Brotherly Bond

My brother and I had a great relationship. When I came into the picture, my dad adopted my brother and gave him our last name, the Roderick last name. He adopted my brother and treated him like his own kid. We were raised together and it was a beautiful situation.

Lessons from an Open Heart

My focus shifted to dealing more with the people I was doing business with at the time, building those relationships and working with them. I was dealing with people who came in, and they wanted to be part of my business. And, if they followed my advice, I would still work with them. But if they were not in the energy of it, it was a simple "No."

It's not just for business; it is my personal life, too. The way I've carried myself as a kid, from friends, to family, to business, to teammates, to coaches, to girlfriends, to whatever it is, that's just how I've carried myself. And I'm pretty happy with the results of my life and how my life has turned out.

I'm not changing. And 99% of the people that know me will tell you I look the same, I act the same, I'm the same free spirit, I'm just getting older. And I say, "Why should I change?" The consistent element is people and you're one side of the relationship with everyone that that involves. I don't play favorites. I don't care about shape, size, color. I've been colorblind my whole life because I'm mixed. I've had every race of friends. My family is mixed. So I don't have any judgment on anybody. I just treat people accordingly. I don't care about the stature, the titles, the money. I'm happy with the way it's been going for me for the last 50 years and I'm not changing.

I've been blessed to have all these different opportunities and different cultures around me. I've seen a lot. So for somebody that doesn't have that access like me, as you see, the world is in a disarray as it is, because of all the hate and all the violence and all the racial tension and all the different things that are going on.

I would tell somebody that doesn't have the opportunity like me to get out in the world and meet people and network and don't have a stereotype and don't have judgment of other people's beliefs and other people's dealing with people. You have to adapt and grow and get your own identity of what the world is based on. Like I said, I'm mixed with all types of people. Probably every race is in my family tree. Most people are really one demographic of their family, so it's hard for them to expand and step out.

I didn't have that boundary because I was raised among some people in my family. So I would just tell somebody, don't base it off your family, your parents, or your friends' beliefs. You have to get out and meet people and see people. And you never know who you're going to meet, who's going to end up being your friend long term, who you're going to end up doing business with because you're opening up and knocking down that barrier to see what people are really about.

You have to get past race, get past the color of someone's skin, get past where somebody comes from, what neighborhood they come from. I learned that from my peers, from being around the world and going into different neighborhoods and doing business with different people. I've always said, "You have to be colorblind."

A Kaleidoscope of Cultures

I have a million stories just because of the different places I've lived, different races of family, be it through marriage or be it through dating or whatever it was. I was able to see all that because my family never really passed judgment on other races. The city of Pomona, when I was raised, was predominantly Black and Hispanic. So from there, you had to adjust because we were living with the Hispanics. You had to know where different territories were. You had to respect each other's boundaries and areas. That's just the way of the land.

And then from there, once Pomona got a little bit more crazy and more active, we moved to the next city over, which was Ontario. And then from Ontario, it was a whole different mix of people. Of course there was a sprinkle of Blacks, depending on what side of the street you went on or what area of Ontario you were in, it was majority Latino, but you had White people, you had Asians starting to come, you had Indians.

And my neighborhood in Ontario, my best friend across the street was Latino. We grew up together, both loving basketball and became entrepreneurs and started a lawn mower business and selling lemonade and had a car wash company together. We liked the same things. I didn't look at him as a Latino kid; he didn't look at me as a Black kid. I would go to his house, he would come to my house, and we ended up being best friends from elementary to right before high school. That was my friend, Glenn.

And then from there around the corner, I had an Indian friend, different culture. You'd take your shoes off and touch the Buddha and eat different foods at his house. But I never looked at him as Indian until later down in life. I'm like, "Damn, I had all these different friends around the corner." I had White friends that we used to skateboard and BMX ride with right around the corner. And that whole neighborhood, I kid you not, there was no animosity, no fighting. Kids would go to and from each other's houses, and have fun. I don't think I had any enemies or fights in that neighborhood. My babysitter was White. She had three White kids that I grew up with, and I never looked at them as White. I just looked at them the same way.

It wasn't normal, but it just *became* normal because all these different families, all these different kids, same age, wherever they came from to move to Ontario, to find a better way of living, cleaner, whatever. Everybody was on the same mission; to have a better life, have better jobs, put their kids in better school districts, and grow. I'm not friends, nor have communications with any of those kids, but I constantly think about them, and I guarantee 90% of them are successful because of the environment and the opportunities that came from living in that area.

When you're surrounded by your own 'tribe,' people with similar passion and goals, you can thrive so much better and be supported. I grew up like that.

Breaking Boundaries and Thriving

On the flip side, now you're living in this environment, you're living in a big house. You've got a backyard, front yard, parents, two-car garage, and living the American dream. So when you go back to the old neighborhood, you hear the rumbling, and you hear the hate, and you hear the people saying, "You think you're better than us." You get that regardless of where you're from and where you're at. You're going to get that. I got that from family, from the kids at school, and later on down the line I got it from the gangs, from my peers that I grew up with and in the industry that, "Oh, you left the neighborhood. You think you're better than everybody."

I don't think I'm better than everybody. My parents took an initiative to give me a better opportunity so I didn't get caught up in all the bullshit that was going on in the neighborhood. I'm thankful for that. And it goes back to say, if my parents didn't do this for me and my brother and themselves, who knows how my life would have turned out. Because some of my cousins and friends didn't have that opportunity. They got caught up in different things because of the environment that they were in. It happens every single day, not just in California, Canada, wherever. It happens; it's just the way of life.

I'm thankful and blessed. The message I want the reader to take out of that is this…

- Look around yourself. What is your environment?

- How is it conducive to what you aspire to?

- Is it going to happen in this environment?

- If not, what are you going to do with it?

You have to be that person who has the willpower to say, "This is not where I want to be, this is not how I want to live. This is not how I want my family to live. I have to do something for myself."

If you're not going to have the resources that I was appointed to have, you have to take that initiative. The people that I deal with now in the industry are the same type of people that have taken the initiative to get out of that environment and try something new. It's working for them. I see it every day, so there's really no excuse.

You might have to struggle when you leave that environment. Because, of course, when you're moving into a better neighborhood or going to a better school, it costs a little more. The cost of living goes up. So you might have to struggle until you get on your feet. But when you struggle and you're going through pains and hunger pains and all that stuff, that's when you appreciate stuff more. That's when you see what it took to get there. And you don't take anything for granted.

Surviving and Rising Above

I tell everybody, "Everybody has problems. Everybody has something going on in their life. Everybody has issues." When people want to give me their sob story and need a shoulder to cry on and all that stuff, I listen. But as soon as they're done, I tell them, "Hey, the strong survive." You have to get past it. There's better days to come. Honestly, and it might be hard to believe, but I'm just living proof. I'm a living testament of it. I haven't had a bad day in 20 years, maybe longer, just because I'm doing the things that I want to do.

Some days are difficult and some days are tougher. I've had some rough times, I've had some tough times, but I've had some good times. I've hit rock bottom two or three times. That's what a lot of people don't know and realize, other than my core family and friends. I've hit rock bottom two or three times: financially, jail, living in motels, hustling, drinking every fucking day, and wondering where my next meal was going to come from, looking over my back. I've had that happen two or three times, all from decisions and pride and ego that put me in those circumstances. And then I came to the realization, "This ain't you." My real friends are like, "Dude, what are you doing? This is not where you're supposed to be."

And you have to suck it up, and you have to get out of that situation. Is it a pride thing? With me, it was a pride thing. Could I have asked for help? Yes. Were certain people offering me help, and I turned it down? Yes. Could I have gone to my parents? Yes. But I had been up, successful; had my ego, and pride, and thought I was hot shit. And then when shit fell off, and I hit rock bottom, I was like, "Damn, you did this to yourself. And you cut off the people that were trying to help you and love you." So it's kind of hard for you to go back and say, "I need help."

A Grandmother's Unwavering Love

But one person that never turned on me when I was down was my grandmother. She's probably one of the few people. Of course my mom was there. At that time, I probably didn't have a cool relationship with my dad, because he was disappointed in some of the things I was doing. Because we're two different kinds of people, but we're the same.

But my grandmother, she never judged me. Was she hurt? Did she know that I had more in me? Of course. Did she judge me? Not once.

I learned from her that judgment has no place, anywhere in my life.

The family (circa 1995)

CHAPTER 5
My Brand; My Legacy

"A few words that describe Big Percy are outgoing, energetic, hustler, grinder, business-oriented, funny, shit-talker, golfer, charismatic. What stands out about him is his willingness to help. If you need to get a plan together, you have something to promote, be a part of something, he always has a positive energy and spirit, mixed with a lot of shit-talking. His mind is always on business: the grind, hustle, but his personality always shines. He has a unique way of making the party better. He lightens up a room with his sarcasm and his humor.

"He's been able to adjust over many years. He's kind of a chameleon from a standpoint of whatever era or whatever room or whatever clientele he needs to educate or communicate with, he can by his versatility in the business space and his grind and his hustle, his relentlessness. A 'no' is not the end. 'No' is just the beginning of finding a way, of finding someone to say 'yes.'

"So, to whoever is reading this, that is what you should do to help yourself advance, absolutely! It's a marathon, not a sprint. He's been able to adapt and change over the years, with business practices, new ways, new technology. He's been hustling for a long time which has been fun to see. My final word is this: I can finally beat him in golf, and he hates it!"
~Matt Barnes

Left to right - Jay Barnes, Matt Barnes, Cordell Broadus, me (circa 2019)

The Barbershop as a Community Hub

There's a barbershop called Groom Time. That was the original place where I did the first meeting for the Pomona City Movement. That barbershop is still, to this day, standing strong and amazing in the city of Pomona. One of the owners played football for my dad at Mt. SAC, and played football with my brother. One of my great friends, a golfing buddy, even though he was a little older than me, we built a relationship throughout the years just because of all the different synergies and different connections. He was and still is my barber.

But now that I have longer hair and braids and everything else, he doesn't do my hair as much, but we still play golf. Our families are connected. His son was a producer for the Pomona City Movement and a lot of those artists. His son does some stuff for me as DJ, some of my events. But the Groom Time Barber Shop, like I said, it's just like the movie *Barbershop*. Yeah, you can get almost anything you want there. It's a great fellowship spot. And it's a great pillar still in the city of Pomona.

Groom Time is owned by Emmett Downs, but we all call him Emmett. Everybody knows him as MD. He owns group homes now and is a great businessman, a great friend. He deals with younger kids and transitioning people from alcoholism and drug abuse. When he first started the group home business, he wanted me to get involved, but it was just something that I didn't do. And I kind of regret it because now he's very successful.

While that ship has sailed on the investment and business side, I've contributed in many ways with clothes and different things and having some of those kids come to different events. But on the business side, yes, that ship has sailed.

Snoop did the Movement that was most prevalent and most important to him, giving back to his city, which was Long Beach. And then from there, it inspired me, the city of Pomona, which Snoop was a part of. And then from there, it's been probably 10, 15 other movements that have spawned from there. We support them in different ways. We post things or comment or give some guidance. He and I both did the ones that were most important to us.

Percy-isms: Wisdom in Action

Along the way, I created some slogans and mantras that I call Percy-isms.

"Don't watch me, watch the moves I make" is one that I got from one of Snoop's uncles.

"We got our own" refers to taking our profitable artist memorabilia-type merchandise to our own companies, and stop making other companies rich off our names.

"Blue and red make green" refers to coming together with people from other various parts, rising above the stereotypes, and doing business together.

"I know where you're from. You know where I'm from."

"We all see the same, and want the same thing."

"We dress the same. We talk the same."

"You're greater in numbers."

There's probably a few others.

Behind the Scenes with Snoop

My first tour, when I got with Snoop, was a six-month tour. It was three months on, came home for a few days, and went back for three months. That was my first introduction to being on the road with Snoop. And from there, I took off. I didn't really have a job title or position, but I did everything. I filled in the blanks. I sat back and analyzed what was missing from his camp and I incorporated it into my daily movement. And then I incorporated the movements into the ancillaries.

Dogg Pound Tour

Innovation on the Road

I love being behind the scenes. I love making plays happen. I started thinking, "There's so much moving and going on that Snoop is missing out on because he doesn't have a point person, a go-to guy. There's so much money that he's missing out that he doesn't even know is floating around. Let me be that connection." On the road we would press up CDs and give them away. And I said, "You know what? That's fine. We'll give some away." And then, "What if we sell these CDs on the road?"

So, I kid you not, we stopped at a gas station on a tour bus and I would take in some CDs. And of course everybody wants to know "Who's on the bus?" Everybody wasn't getting off the bus, but I would get off the bus because I would have to go get different supplies. Snoop can't get off the bus everywhere we fucking stop. That's just a gift.

I was the point person and everywhere we stopped for gas and food and whatever, I would take the CDs. At the end, after I got everything, I would tell whoever was in the store or the people behind the register, "Snoop's on the bus. Do you want to buy this CD?" Whoever, wherever we were, they would buy. So then I'd go back on the bus and I'd have sold 30 CDs on consignment.

Tour bus life (circa 2010)

I started doing that everywhere. Then when it got big, I said, "You know what? What if I get Snoop to sign them?" That led to us selling people pictures of themselves with Snoop. At one stop, we had over a thousand people chasing us at the mall. Snoop would take off a shirt and throw it in the corner, and I'd grab it and sell it. We invited people backstage and sold them merch. All these things brought a lot of money; wherever I saw an opportunity, we capitalized on it.

Laying the Blueprint for the Industry

And those things that we did early on have now translated into real ancillary businesses. Not just for Snoop but other artists, the younger artists that watch the things that we did. They have now incorporated that into their business model and their business blueprint. And they're doing some of the things that we started on our early tour days. They're now using them on their tour days.

A perfect example is Chris Brown who now is doing Meet & Greets and charging $1,000 doing all these crazy pictures with his fans and everything else backstage. And that's something that we started doing in the early 2000s.

These artists do that, you can come backstage, meet them, take a picture, get some merch, get a ticket to the concert, get a ticket to the after party. These are some things that we did early on and now have trickled down to our younger homies in the entertainment business.

All genres of music do it now. Nobody was really doing it like that. I'm not going to say we were the first, but I guess we were the first in our demographic, in our genre. Snoop is the Godfather, so you have every genre looking at what he does. And they pay homage and let us know throughout our journeys that a lot of things that we did early on, they're now doing it too.

I guess that's why they call us Unc. We're proud of them, watching our 'nieces' and 'nephews' grow.

The Pomona City Movement

Snoop was able to deal with all the different crip sets in his area. He did something very powerful, and put together this thing called the Long Beach City Movement where he gave an opportunity to all the up and coming artists in the city of Long Beach a chance to work with him. He would help you produce some music, and we would take the top tier selection of artists on tour.

It went viral. The news picked it up. And when he did that, he said, "P, what are you going to do next?" I said, "It's only right for me to start and promote a Pomona City Movement." I went to my neighborhood, the Hub, the barbershop, where 99% of all African American hubs are, and set up the first meeting. The barbershop is a place where you lay your guns down, no bullshit, because kids and older people are in there.

Building Unity Across Communities

All the different crips sections and two or three representatives from the bloods (the bloods were not able to move around like that in the city – they really had to stay in their own section) showed up to work together in harmony. Of course we heard the backlash of the different levels. You had the BGs, which were the baby gangsters. Then you had the OGs, which were the original gangsters. Then you had the double OGs, which were the older OGs, and then you had the triple OGs that sat down with the gang bang grandfathers. So of course you were hearing all the different backlashes and the rumors and all the hate from the sidelines.

But we did manage to put it together and we took those kids out on a two-month tour and paid them, got them out of the neighborhood, and that movement, probably going on about 8 to 10 years ago now, is still having positive effects.

Snoop had to step away because he didn't want to feel like he was playing favoritism to more kids from his neighborhood than the other parts of Long Beach and vice versa. I had to do the same thing. So we stepped away. Other cities have since started movements based off of what Snoop and I did. Those kids that we reached are still working, still doing other things, starting their own movements.

Transforming Lives Through Music

I still talk to a lot of artists and tell them, "I'm going to tell you the truth. If your music sucks, I'm going to tell you. But you might be talented behind the camera. You might be better at making the beats. You have to find your niche." And I don't sugarcoat shit. I tell it like it is. That's why they respect it. That's why I'm so respected in the game.

Many of those guys have now evolved into producers, started film companies, or taken on management roles, even though they initially thought they were destined to be rappers. Now they're managing some younger kids in their neighborhood. So it spawned off into a great situation.

Those movements are going. And big time artists have been discovered from a lot of these different movements. We were just laying the blueprint of what we knew, what it took to make it. And we've given these guys the opportunity to get some of our guidance. I point people in the right direction.

People getting on a tour bus, having never been on one, they had never left their city, never seen snow before, never seen that many White people before, never seen that many Latinos, never knew there were so many Latinos in Texas and Arizona and New Mexico. Tasting different foods. It was a bigger world for them.

We were giving these artists guidance on what to do when they came together. "You're both from the city. You're the best rapper over here, and you're the best rapper over there. Do a song together." So when I started to promote a city movement, it was in the newspaper. Gang violence went down 40%. My grandmother cut out the clippings.

Snoop Youth Football League

When Snoop started the Snoop Youth Football League, the city of Pomona didn't have football for over 25 years because they cut out all the after-school activities. They cut out all the YMCAs and the boys' clubs and all the extracurricular things that you could do after school. They cut all that out. So what do you think you're going to do? Go in the streets, go to the park, watch the gang members, and now that's your family. So Snoop was the new Pop Warner. It decreased the violence in the gangs by 30 something percent throughout the city of Los Angeles

Entrepreneurship in Entertainment

My cousin Sugar Bear, Terence Flowers, is the founder of Power House Records, which is the biggest record label to come out of the city of Pomona. I was able to form our management company, which was 7 South Entertainment with another affiliation from the city of Pomona. (When I say affiliation, I'm just speaking about gang life and another facet of what we know as street culture). C-note was my business partner and is from another part of town, which was called 357, which was gang life.

Me with Sugar Bear (circa 2004)

We formed 7 South Entertainment Management Group as a collaboration with Power House Records. The "7" represents our collective identity, while "South" signifies my roots on the south side of Pomona. To this day, the connection we built within the city remains strong—not based on gang ties, but on unity and collaboration. The bond between both sides of Pomona continues to be relevant, fostering a sense of community and mutual respect that endures.

RMM came after 7 South. But it doesn't exist on the magnitude it did back in the '90s. It's probably 50% of the unity that's still going on and the relevance of the two sides of the community in the city of Pomona.

Even when I started the Pomona City Movement, those factors had a great relationship, and they still do, but the "7 South Management" doesn't exist like that anymore. Now everything is filtered through RMM. But I still do have one of the business cards from 7 South Management. I have it in my office frame.

7 South Management business card

My journey into entrepreneurship really began as an evolution out of solving a dilemma. I began to notice that the companies that made the products that would have a celebrity's likeness or endorsement on them made the lion's share of the proceeds from selling those products, while the people whose names were selling them were ending up with table scraps. I saw it happening to Snoop Dogg in particular. I said, "Hey, let's make our own," and so we did.

Strategic Partnerships

I consulted with a brand called Belaire Champagne. When they first got into the business, I not only consulted with them, but also linked them up with different celebrities and artists and then from there the relationship expanded with those different people, and deals were made.

I've worked with Channel 11 News, which is out here on the west coast, called Fox News. I built a big relationship with the main news lady at Fox. I was a fan of hers as a kid and then got the pleasure of working with her and growing with her throughout the years and bringing her a part of a lot of our different events and projects and newsworthy information. I always give her the inside scoop and I always give her first dibs on covering what's happening. That's Christine Devine with Fox News in California.

And then there's one of the biggest radio stations on the west coast, which is KDay. It's one of the biggest radio stations and I have dealt with all the radio hosts, all the disc jockeys for years. I bring them our new music and artists and do interviews with them. I was able to meet the managers of the company and I've built those relationships. It's just continuously helping each other grow.

The Art of Good Business

I have great relationships with Mel's Diner, the restaurant. It grew from us pulling our cars up there with my Rider Gang and my car club and now they sponsor a lot of my events.

Rider Gang Car Club as featured on Jay Leno's tv show (2021)

I do different things, and it's just built off relationships, doing good business, interacting and finding out who the owners or the managers are and then cross-promoting and cross-networking their brands with my clientele and my Rolodex.

There's just so many; I have so many great relationships with various different business owners. There used to be The Staple Center. Now, it's the big arena where the Lakers and Clippers play. I have great relationships now with COFI and The Chargers Organization. It's pretty much anybody that I come in contact with that has a great business, great product, great merchandise, I just cut through the chase and build a relationship with the owners or the managers or the employees and then we do business.

Trusting Intuition in Business

There are definitely some people I steer away from. It has something to do with my upbringing. I'm a Leo, so I don't really give people two or three strikes. It's usually just one strike with me and if I'm not feeling it in my gut, I don't deal with them. I don't care if the money's good. We have a saying out here: "all money's not good money." Just going off the vibe and the energy of somebody, I will not do it. It doesn't matter what the specific vibe is, if it's not a good vibe, I'm done. I've done that several times and passed on some large amounts of money just because I knew it was going to be a headache or some bullshit later dealing with these people or their company.

There are many red flags. If I'm dealing with an owner and I pick up on energy that feels shady or fast-talking, I take that seriously. I have so many relationships, so I can reach out to other people to ask about their past dealings with these owners, brands, and everything else. If I get trustworthy information from someone I respect, I won't deal with them. It doesn't matter how good the opportunity seems— once I've got the backstory from credible people, I step back. I've missed out on plenty of money by turning these situations down, but in the long run, my name stays clear. I won't risk getting caught up in legal trouble or headaches down the road. I'd rather walk away.

Supporting Young Entrepreneurs

I'm looking to connect with a good vibe, good business, good products, great energy, great employees, and family-oriented. I love dealing with family-oriented businesses, minority businesses, and upstart businesses. I love dealing with young entrepreneurs because if I get a hold of it at the beginning on the incubation side and then I can watch it blossom and grow, I get a lot of joy and excitement out of that.

The way I deal with an upstart is by researching them, checking their socials, getting feedback from friends and the streets and other colleagues about this upstart brand or this particular artist. From there, I'll do my due diligence and then from there, if I want to work with that particular brand or artist or client, I'll just do it off the cuff. I'll just do it off the strength, the love and connect them into my circle, into my world, because a lot of the things and a lot of people out here on the West Coast, I just want to see them succeed, see them win.

I'm not looking for any monetizing and financial gain, let alone from the beginning of the relationship. I just want everybody on the West Coast, regardless of color, race, ethnicity, where they're from; I do it for the love of them. If they have a great brand, their spirit, nine times out of ten, they've been getting at me for a long time either via seeking me out and about, social media, texting me and just them being consistent doing *that,* I just do it on the love for them, wanting them to win. Then, I always express myself to people, and people know how I get out and how I work.

I play the game fair. If I did something, and it grew, and it came into something and made some money, I feel in my heart and my spirit that they'll do the right thing and take care of me financially. If it does something on a major scale, from there, if it's growing, and big things are happening, then we'll get into some kind of a written agreement.

I find that it usually means they're approaching me and my name and my business strategy and my business motto. It speaks for itself. And for me to even take a liking to someone, to deal with somebody, they had to crack my barrier for me to even open up to them. So they already know how to get in.

And I have such a great infrastructure, and security wall with all the different people that work for me and work with me. They sift through the bullshit before it even gets to me. They're my team. Yeah, all those people that work for me and deal with me and have a role in my life and in my company, they have now turned into family. I have had a core of five for the last 20 years. And then from the last 15 years, I probably have a core of seven. And then probably for the last 10 years, I have a max, about 10 core people that I deal with.

Staying Relevant in the Game

Why I still do what I'm doing, still staying relevant is that it ties into the essence of who Big Percy is. People still love me today after 25, 30 years of doing this business. I think that, honestly, I know people still want to deal with me. And, you know, they call me up for a reason. And I don't take that lightly, people calling me Uncle, or I've been a father figure to them. I've either dealt with their family members or parents, and now it's trickling down to me dealing with them, because they're artists now. And it's just the genuine love that people have for me, because I don't sugarcoat shit. I'm a straight shooter. There's no in-between with me. It's either you love me or you hate me.

When I say they hate me, they hate me because I keep it real. And that's what keeps me relevant, because I don't sugarcoat anything to anybody. I don't care. It can be Obama down to the lowest person on the totem pole. I treat everybody the same, and if it's wrong, it's wrong.

> *"If it walks like a duck and it's quacking, it's a duck."*

It's nothing else. I can't change it. You can't change it. That's what it is. And I keep it very, very straight and to the point with everybody; the point of being right or wrong. If it's the pros and cons, I've done everything that I can for somebody.

An example of me keeping it straight to the point is if an artist gets at me and says, "I'm trying to get in the business. I need you to manage me. I need you to get me to Snoop. I need all this." I'm going to tell them from the beginning, "This could happen. It's a potential," *or* I'm going to tell them, "You're not ready. The time's not right. I'm not going to waste your time. And you're not going to waste mine."

Get straight to the point and ask me what you want me to do. I'm either going to tell you I can't do it or I'm going to tell you you're not ready to do it. But if I *can*, I can do it 100% of the time; it's *going* to get done. There may be other people I can guide you to. But if I can't do it, I don't want you wasting my time. I don't want you calling me a hundred times.

In this entertainment business, it goes a long way, because it's a rarity. A lot of people are in it for themselves, looking out for themselves and lying to people and just telling people anything for them to try to get personal gain. In my case, it would make that relationship really, really short. It would make it short because I have to cut you off. You're not in it for a genuine purpose. I look at everybody the same when it comes to really doing good business. No matter what means they come with, what name they come with, what popularity, whatever, it means nothing because I've seen everything. I say it all the time. I've seen everything but Christ. And I'm not trying to see Him anytime soon!

Sometimes on initial approaches and meeting me, if I didn't have the vibe, and they came back later where they have changed their ways, done what I suggested, now I'm considering 100% if the vibe is right.

If it's a young artist, and at a particular time they don't have their stuff ready, I'm going to tell them and give them my opinion and my advice. If they take it and go one year after the other, that's on them. But if they take it and use it and implement it into their daily practices, then I can observe and watch and see and get feedback from the world or watch their Instagram, and they're implementing that into their daily rituals to try to improve, 100 percent I'll deal with them on a later basis.

That's happened many times because I can tell a lot of brands that if they want to deal with Snoop, this is what it's going to take. Don't penny pinch, don't nickel and dime. If I get you to the table with him, and your deal or your brand is bullshit, he's going to see through it. And he's gonna tell me he's not fucking with you. And once it gets to that point, and then I try to revisit and bring you back, it might be too late.

But if you come to me, and ask for my information, and I consult you, and you get it done, and you meet it to my qualifications, and then I bring you to the table, now you got something.

The Connector and the Buffer

A lot of people actually consider me a buffer, a connector for a lot of my clients, and a lot of the brands that I deal with, because they know, I'm going to tell them the real deal; I'm going to tell them what it takes. If you don't have it, that's fine. Go back, spend some more time, get it together and come back. If you have it and you're ready, I'm going to take you to the table. And now it's time for you to close. I got you to the water; I can't force you to drink. But if you do drink, I'll give you your next sip, your next whatever. And if you take that drink, you're going to be fulfilled, nourished and everything else after that.

Expanding the Brand

My brand is expanding every day. I always come across different deals and different people around the world that have ideas that they want to pitch to me. Of course they want to pitch it to me now that my company and my name stand alone; they want to pitch different ideas and different concepts and different deals for my clients so that's never ending.

I'm working on so many different things today with Snoop and Matt Barnes. It's just because I've done so much good business with people. They always want to come back on some residual and some longevity-type of deals so they always reach out to me.

CHAPTER 6

Passing the Torch

"Big Percy is a dominant force to be reckoned with. He always came in, and he was the life of the party. He always brightened up things, always put a smile on your face. That is Percy. He is a leader and he's a great host too, great concierge. With those two deadly combinations, it always equaled the recipe for success. "Percy has been very instrumental in a lot of people's careers. He did a lot of stuff for Snoop, and was the intricate part of his game, even from a financial point of view. He always runs the bag, that's what you notice about Percy.

"When you're coming up and earning your stripes in this game, there are a lot of people who are going to hate you, but that's just the process that every person must go through moving from a street hustler to an entrepreneur. He definitely paid the cost to be his own boss, like we say, 'we got our own,' and seeing his elevation from the place where we love, Pomona, California, it's just surreal, but I'm not surprised; that's Percy.

"He's a blessing to the game and it's good to see him make his business pivot to be able to ride on his own, as his own brand because he's definitely been selfless in regards to

helping others, whether it's for money or for connections. I have a lot of love from him as well. I was there at the right time for him and all these people from our neighborhood to be able to bring them around at a time when we're doing platinum records over there at Snoop Dogg's old house and he just fit. He's always got my voice and I'm happy to be a part of his success.

"When you read this book, it will give you inspiration, or if you have inspiration it'll elevate your motivation, it'll elevate your drive. It's the good, the bad, and the ugly rolled up into one. He's definitely been the victor in this rap game, and the music game in general so when you read this book it's going to inspire you, fire you, and it's going to elevate you at the same time." ~Kokane

Me with Kokane

The Facade of Glamour

I make things look easy and glamorous and fun, but, a lot of those things, heartaches and trials and tribulations, I've actually probably hit rock bottom two or three times in my life. I've made several mistakes. But a lot of people wouldn't know about that because of the way I carry myself and the way I dress and intermingle with people.

I was able to correct the mistakes I made in the past. Some people probably don't know that story. I know that a journey that pertains to making some bad decisions and hanging out with the wrong people, trying to make some fast money and hustling, there's a few ways that it can end. And a couple of those times it didn't end well for me.

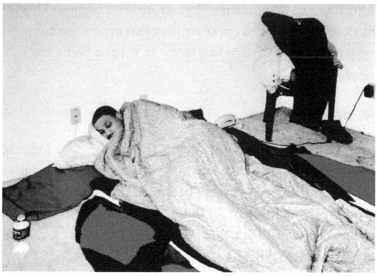

This is me hustlin' and waitin' "TRAP HOUSE" (circa 1999)

Hitting Rock Bottom

One time in jail, it was with the grace of God and my financial backing from my father and the support system I had that I was able to obtain some great lawyers and everything was resolved, so I was cleared of those charges because I didn't do it. A couple other times, I made some decisions and spent some time in jail, didn't take care of some responsibilities and didn't finish my court obligations and that stuff backfired.

I had to do about eight more months another time. But all my last encounters, in my late 20s, early 30s, I haven't seen a jail cell since. And I don't plan on seeing one ever again. That wasn't me and that's not where I was supposed to be.

A lot of people use jail as an excuse and fall back into the same bullshit that they did to get themselves in there the first time instead of making a pivot and adjusting. I was fortunate because I had a major support system. And I had opportunities that others are not privileged to have. It definitely was a major factor in me not going back in those directions.

The System's Grip

If you don't have a good support system or access to good legal services and you end up in jail, just like anything, you'll be caught in the system. If a kid's parents mess up, they're caught in the system and have to go into foster care. And it's hard for them to get out. Just like the homeless situation. If they don't have means and they're out on the street, then that's when the mental health issues happen.

It's the same in the legal system. If you get caught in the legal system, if you don't have the means for a great legal, you're caught up, and you're going to end up getting what they give you, which is a public defender, and they don't care. The public defender and other lawyers and judges all sit in the same room during lunchtime and determine people's fate. So with those circumstances against people, it's a hard, hard road.

And that's why a lot of people, once they're faced with those adversities, end up taking deals and taking time that they know that they're not supposed to be given, but they just don't have the resources to fight it. And instead of prolonging it, they go ahead and take the time. And then once you're in the system, hopefully it's not the prison system. Jail and prison are two different things.

But once you get into that prison system, it's really hard for someone to make it out, because now you're faced with all the different circumstances and heartaches that happen in the prison system that can force you to catch more time, get caught up, and then your mentality is definitely shattered once you're in that system. And then if you come out, and you still don't have the support, and you still don't have the resources, that's where a lot of people get sucked right back in. It's sad because some of these guys are innocent, but they don't have the means and the resources to fight it.

A lot of people just stay away from the services that are available to them because there are so many people waiting for them and they don't have any faith in those different organizations because of the time factor, how many different people they're dealing with, how many other people's cases they're working on, and by the time they get to you, it's too late.

Inequality in Sentencing

It definitely comes at the higher level based upon these different laws, and a lot of the guys that I'm speaking of, the laws pertain to drug offenses and gang activity and stuff like that. Now, with marijuana and weed becoming a little more lenient and legal, those cases are now being revisited, and some of those guys are getting less time or getting released. That's happened over the last few years. But in LA and on the West Coast, they make it harder for Black men because they know the majority of the Black men are involved with gangs, involved in drug sales and everything else, so they group them together. They run people's cases out here a little differently, because if you're a gang member selling drugs and caught with a gun, now you're pretty much fucked.

When other people get those same charges, and even though they're not in the gang, they get the same charges. Same things happen, same amount of drugs, and they get a little less sentencing and less time because they're not a gang member, and that doesn't go just for Black gang members, that goes for Mexican gang members, all gang members, and that's pretty much what all young males in California on the West Coast are privy to because that's just the nature of the neighborhoods they live in, and it's difficult.

Breaking the Cycle

I had a friend that just got out of jail after doing 12 years. He came out, all the friends that he ran with are doing well now, raising their family, business owners, not doing any of the things that they were doing when he first went in. He came out for less than two weeks. He still had to protect himself, he still had to struggle and strive, and he was trying to figure out a way. He got caught back up and back in the system just on one dumb move.

It's not that he actually was discouraged; it's just the circumstances of how he was living and how he had to protect himself. The ways of his mind got him caught up. He was doing the right things, and just one bad move, now he's back in, and that's less than two weeks. These stories are constant, and then it just came to a point of how I was living and the things I was doing I could have easily been in those same kinds of circumstances. But I wanted better for myself.

A Shared Journey

It could have been me, it could have been Snoop, it could have been my cousins, it could have been damn near everybody that I associate with now, fall into the same circumstances, the same roles that I did, just different parts of the city and different cases and different situations. Pretty much everybody I know, work with, deal with, associate with, pretty much has the same story. All these guys, and that's why we bond, gel, fellowship, work together, do business together, and our families hang out with each other. Because we all have the same story.

But we all wanted something better, and it clicked at a point in time in our heads, in our minds. Hopefully, with the support and not hurting your family members, and disappointing your mothers and grandmothers, everybody that I deal with now hit that turning point and said, this is not what they wanted to be, and wanted to become a productive part of society. And now those same people, from Snoop, to everybody, The Dogg Pound, and my cousins, and everyone, are fathers, and successful businessmen, and great pillars in their community.

Inspiration Through Action

I'm a living testimony, an inspiration, so if you can look at me, and see the things I'm doing, and the way I'm moving, and you know I came from the same streets, and the same blocks, and the same heartaches that you come from, and I decided to change my life, you have to look at that as inspiration.

That's all I can really do, and keep pushing the narrative, and keep showing you there's a better way. So this is preaching to the choir, and doing all this other stuff, it's cool, but I don't see that working. Like I said, it's bigger than me; it's the system, and the best thing I can tell a young person is don't ever get caught up in the system, because once you're in the system, it's hell to get out. And when a policeman or a judge looks at your past record, even though they're not supposed to judge you on that, and stereotype you, it's just human nature. If you carry yourself as a decent human being early in life, and don't get caught up in the system, now you've got a fighting chance.

Every day, I think I'm helping people by living my lifestyle, and doing what I do to put out a positive message, and living my life carefree, headache free. That's how I think I'm helping people, because I hear it every day from phone calls, text messages, social media, bumping into people saying, "Big P, you're an inspiration." "Big P, thanks for doing what you're doing, keeping the culture alive," ...x, y, z.

A Vessel for Opportunity

I like to put people in better situations. I let them come into my world and see things that I know they'll never be able to see on their own, and once again, if you can't take that as an inspiration and an opportunity and a platform for you to springboard yourself into some different situations, then this is maybe not for you.

A lot of people that I've brought around, put around Snoop, and put in the studios, took them on trips, or put them in rooms with executives, some have parlayed it into other situations and networked with those same people, and done some great things with it. That's what I'm used for.

I'm a vessel and I've always been a vessel for people.

The Business of Incarceration

You see, the United States is totally different from Canada and totally different from other countries. Our prison and jail system, incarceration system, juvenile hall system is a multi-billion dollar operation. So they don't want to build more schools and more recreational centers and more places for kids and keep them off the streets. They'd rather build more jails and penitentiaries because it's such a money-maker.

It's very sad and I honestly don't see any hope. I just see a spinning cycle and it's been going on for years. It's based off where you live and your environment.

The Impact of Environment

I have been blessed to move around and get out of certain situations before things got bad for me and my family. And that has played a major factor because when I walk out the door, I see hope. I see better living. I see productive people. I see productive things. It's cleaner. It's nicer. Those things play a major factor in a kid's upbringing and a kid's mental health.

Even as an adult, when I drive and go into certain situations in neighborhoods, it's sad to say, but it is depressing because there's no hope. You're looking at the drug addicts. You're looking at the homelessness. You're looking at the structures that are not kept up and not taken care of. All you see is the police and hear sirens and everything else. That plays a major role on the mental health of a person, young or old.

Escaping the Inner-City Cycle

That's where I have been blessed throughout my life, seeing two parents, being around my grandmother, seeing my aunties, seeing my uncle, seeing the family structure, my family owning homes and land and everything else. Those were positive reinforcements. My dad working every day, my mom working every day, food in the house, a nice car, being able to go to the park and not have to worry about fighting and shootouts and everything else.

Those things play a major role in somebody's upbringing and mental well-being. It changes the path of a person's life immensely. I see it every day. And that's when, if you're a star athlete coming out of the inner city or someone sees some talent in you, it's usually a grandparent or some kind of family member, or even in the streets, a hustler or somebody that has some money, they take a liking to that kid or that person that has some talent. And the first thing they want to do is hopefully get them out of that situation, get them into a different school, put them in some camps or different projects so they can thrive.

Opportunities Through Sports

Those opportunities are few and far between, but it does happen. It happened for me in sports. And it happened for me with my parents moving us out of those different environments every time they saw things getting bad. I was able to travel and see a lot of things and have opportunities. I didn't have to just play in the inner city parks and everything. I traveled the world playing basketball, which led me to opportunities, getting a scholarship and everything else. A lot of people don't have those opportunities coming out of the ghetto and the inner city.

CHAPTER 7

Making My Way

"My experience with Big Percy, the legend, the man, the myth himself; it's been about four and a half years since I've known him personally but I've watched him be successful at not only running his own personal business but beginning and starting, from the ground up, his liquor company with True Legacy Vodka and then I've played a part significantly in actually helping him get his marijuana strain, the Don P, into a few shops. So I just want to give a lot of praise, a lot of honor to Big Percy for his perseverance, for his support for the West Coast and for the culture. He has not only been someone who has been an inspiration to a lot of artists but he's also been someone who's been there to support, help and guide a lot of artists and up-and-coming talent in the Los Angeles and Southern California area to success.

"Big Percy, in my life today, is not only a mentor but also a great help in assisting me in creating my businesses and my future projects. So, the best thing I can say is, 'Congratulations Big Percy for everything you've got going. We're proud of you. You make the city proud. You make the state proud and we look forward to seeing the many more great things you have coming in the future.'

~Jeff California Jones, 25 years in the music industry, connected with Big Percy through his music. Jeff is now the A&R for RMM, the record label that Percy runs. He has executive produced the second Rider Gang as well as Big Percy's personal album, '50 Years of P,' and co-written all of his music that he's released including 'We Got Our Own' and 'Order My Vodka.'

Me with Jeff California Jones

A Mother's Resilience and Unwavering Dedication

My mom was there every single day, rain, sleet or snow, working long hours, doing what she had to do. I had financial support and everything from my dad, but everything that I learned and saw on a daily basis was a Black woman providing for her two kids and keeping us out of trouble and showing up to everything. That's what I remember of my mom. She still does it for me, for my kids, for the whole family. Most kids, if they don't grow up with two parents, it's sad to say, the mom or the dad is on drugs or not working or alcoholic or abusive and everything else. Those things play a major factor on a kid's upbringing.

The love was there, the providing was there, the discipline was there, the structure was there, you know, all those things were there, from my entire family.

The Influence of My Father and the Roots of My Basketball Passion

My dad wasn't a basketball player; he was a track and field athlete, and football was his claim to fame. His other claim to fame was coaching football. He was a bowling guy, bowling instructor, softball, and all those different things. But the love of basketball came from watching my older cousin play, who was one of the top basketball players in the nation. He probably goes down to this day as maybe one of the top three basketball players that ever came out of my city. And the high school he went to is the high school that I dreamed of going to.

A Dream Deferred for a Safer Path

But my dad didn't let me or my brother go there because it was in the ghetto (in his eyes, not our eyes, because that's where we were born and raised). It was just in the city of Pomona, Gary High School, and it was known for basketball, sports, putting out top athletes, but you had to make a decision, were you going to be a top athlete, or were you going to get pulled into the street life?

And a lot of those guys that were the top stars and athletes got pulled into the street life. Like I said, my cousin and me being young, going to his game and his team was tops in our area. And actually a couple of players made it to the NBA, another player who played on my cousin's team ended up going and playing for the Kansas Jayhawks and won a national championship. I watched these guys as a kid, doing high flying stuff, and it was just all Black guys on the team, striving.

Falling in Love with Basketball

That's where my love of basketball came from. And then I just took it upon myself as I started getting taller and growing. I would go play with the older guys all the time. I played in the neighborhood, I played in my front yard. Everywhere I lived, my parents always had a basketball court for me on the garage or in the backyard. Because they knew how much I loved basketball; I played it all day and all night.

The Journey Through High School and Travel Ball

I went to different parks, traveling. And then I had the opportunity to go to decent schools that had decent basketball programs. And I started making a name for myself and was able to play on one of the top travel basketball programs in Southern California with several guys that made it to the NBA. It was amazing. And I played on one of the top high school basketball teams in the area. And then from there, due to academic things and some things that I brought on myself, I had to go through the junior college route, which was a blessing in disguise for me. I had many scholarship offers right out of high school, but I just didn't do the things that I needed to do, testing wise and everything else, to transfer. I went the junior college route and still got a top scholarship and was able to play a little professional basketball as well.

I stuck with it and knew that was going to be a way for me to make a name. I always knew I was making a basketball career. I didn't make it at the highest level like I could have (due to me, not anybody else). I don't blame anybody but myself looking back at it. But I always knew that I would go far in sports and everybody knew that I would be in some kind of entertainment aspect. And that's what I'm still doing. It's a blessing.

My cousin's name is George Hardin, also known as Sir Dunk A Lot, or Andre, as we called him. Back in the day, I played travel basketball with the number one team in Southern California, the American Roundball Association, or ARC. Our main rival was Slamma Jam. It was simple— you were either with Slamma Jam or with ARC.

The reason I played ARC was because in my eyes, at a young age, I knew youth sports was becoming a business. The guy that ran ARC had money. He had sponsorship, nicer uniforms, nicer shoes, and he happened to be White. And the other guy that ran Slamma Jam happened to be Black. And I just made a decision that I wanted to play with the nicer things, the better things and everything else, which bred and led to, I'd say, having a nicer and better place. My junior year I was ranked number 10 as the best small forward in the state of California.

Playing with Legends: Jason Kidd, Kevin Ollie, and the ARC Experience

My point guard was Jason Kidd, who is the NBA Olympic champion, and now is the head coach of the Dallas Mavericks. The other star point guard on the team was Kevin Ollie, NBA for over 14 years, college champions at Connecticut, and still coaching at a high level in the NBA.

And it's probably two or three other guys that made it to the NBA, spent some time in the NBA, but the top two guys in my eyes that were on that team were Jason Kidd and Kevin Ollie. They were ranked number one guards at that time. And a lot of those guys, Jason Kidd, Kevin Ollie, Monty Buckley, I'm still friends with to this day, got all their numbers in my phone. We chat, we congratulate each other, we see each other out and about. I'd say it's a powerful brotherhood.

Me with Jason Kidd

We went 39 and 0 that year, and didn't lose a game. Traveling from Vegas to Arizona to Virginia, wherever the top tournaments were, we went and we won them. I had an opportunity. They'll tell you I was probably the most athletic person, the best athlete on that team, but I didn't conform as much as they did. And I didn't play the system and play the role as much as they did. I was more of a rebel.

Rebel Tendencies and Hard Lessons on the Court

If anything happened on that team or any trouble arose or any fights broke out, I was probably in the mix or started it, which probably led to me not making it and taking it as far as I could have. I've accepted that. I also had an opportunity to play on the B Team of that organization. And that team could have been mine and I could have been the star player on that team. But, like I said, as a young kid, I understood the business and I understood being on the A Team, even if I didn't play as much as I thought I would, I'm still going to get all the looks because that's who all the coaches and scouts are coming to see, the A Team.

And all I have to do is a certain few things that I know I can do. And I'm still going to get the opportunity to receive top offers and top scholarships. So I understood the business aspect at a young age.

A Starting Five to Remember

Going back to my high school team, our starting five at my high school. At that time it was unheard of, but my starting five at my high school all received division one scholarships. So from the point guards to the centers, if you started on my high school team, we all received division one scholarships. And right now this area is a little different because there's more opportunities with social media, more travel ball teams and youth sports and everything is now a huge business. It was unheard of then.

So yeah, my high school basketball team, starting was me, Michael Jackson, Carlton Oliver, Marcus Bell.

Mentoring Athletes and the Love of the Game

Even though I don't play basketball, I watch it. I critique it. I know the top high school players, anything I can do to mentor an athlete that I see, I take that opportunity to do it.

And I think all those things have, of course, filtered down into my daughter's life and how I raised her and how I've been a part of her life through the game and the love of basketball.

A Father's Tough Love: Coaching My Daughter

My daughter just finished her first year of college basketball at the same college I went to. As a freshman, she was voted defensive player of the year. She made MVP of a tournament as a freshman. The team she started on was, at the time, the top team in Southern California and the top team in California. She started on that team as a freshman and she made second team all conference as a freshman. She has done some things that I wasn't able to do as a freshman at my same college. She has already surpassed me.

And I considered myself at that time a great athlete, but she just surpassed me. I coached her as a youth and it just came to a point that the outside, which was my parents and other family members, said I was too tough on her. And I was. It was hard because all her early basketball and development came from me.

That was an opportunity when she came to stay with me and visit me. That was our bonding. And it still is. It's crazy how basketball plays a part in our life and my family, sports in general, but that was bonding time for her and I. Go outside, play basketball, go over some skills, give her some training, watch her development, see the joy she had when I gave her praises and everything when she did stuff right. I saw so much in her, so much natural ability. And I saw so much of me in her and things and the way she grasped the game, it was magical. So I wanted to pull it out of her as much as I could. I was asked to either take it easier on her, which I wasn't going to do, or not coach her.

So I stepped away from coaching her and then I put her in the right positions, in the right places, the right schools and the right trainers. And I stepped away, which was a blessing, but it was difficult. I did it because I wanted the best for her.

I think she loved it because that's when we bonded and that's when we spent the most time together and she saw the joy I had in coaching her. I think she enjoyed it, but I was getting criticism from the other family, grandma, grandpa, and other people that just saw how tough I used to be on her.

She was my daughter and she was better than everybody. And she was, and like I told her, and I tell her to this day and I tell other kids that I deal with and work with, if you didn't have the 'it' factor, I would tell you. But if you have 'it,' it's my job as a coach or a mentor to pull it out because I don't want you to waste that talent. And my daughter had the impact. She still has the impact. When you have an impact, there are things that are just natural. It can't be coached. It can't be taught. They have it. And those are the ones that make it, and to this day, she has that effect. It can be pulled out and refined by the right coach.

The 'It' Factor: Recognizing True Talent

Her coaches see the same qualities I've seen in her. They've seen the same 'it' factors, the same qualities that I've seen and they pulled them out. And that's why she is at the top. She was able to succeed as a freshman in college, a true 18-year old freshman to do some of the things that she did.

The 'it' factor is in everything, not just sports; it's in entertainment, music, everything. A perfect example is when Snoop and Young Sagg put the Long Beach City Movement together, which was to bring all the different musical aspects and the young and up and coming artists out of the city of Long Beach. And then I followed and did the same thing with the city of Pomona. There were so many different talented kids that we were able to take on their first national tour of seeing the road, getting paid, doing shows.

And I had to tell a lot of those guys, "Some of you are not going to make it. Some of you are going to be better as producers and writers. Some of you guys are going to be better as managers or camera people."

Facing Hard Truths and Tough Conversations

I'm the one that has to tell them the truth. And I've done it for many, many years. I don't sugar coat anything. If you're coming to me and asking me for advice and want me to manage you and mentor you, I'm going to tell you the truth.

And some of those people that I told that are now managers and producers and camera people, and they're being successful at that as well. Do they still have love for the music? Yes. Are they still producing and making music? Yes. But are they using their qualities and skills and everything else to do some of the things that I've guided them into and now making a profit and being profitable? Yes. Because I don't want anyone's time wasted and don't want them to miss out on an opportunity in something else.

It's definitely a Debbie Downer moment. "Unc is tripping, Unc is on bullshit, Unc is hating," or whatever comes out of it. But as time goes on, months and years later, and reality hits, nine times out of ten, they come back and say, "Damn, Unc, you were right. Damn, Unc, you saw something in me I didn't see in myself. I appreciate you, I love you for that. Nobody else ever told me that."

Leaving Basketball Behind

Sharing this news piece:

> ### "UOP Basketball
>
> *The University of Pacific basketball player Damien Roderick was suspended from the team indefinitely, according to Coach Bob Thomason. No reason for the dismissal was announced.*

Roderick, a 6-foot-5 sophomore forward, transferred to UOP after sitting out last year. He played at Mt. San Antonio College as a freshman and averaged 10 points and 6.3 rebounds per game."

Damn crazy part is, I had been suspended at every level of basketball at some point since I was a kid, from pee wee ball to Pomona Youth League AAU Junior High and overseas. Damn, I was a fool but I say that to say that God, Jah, had a bigger, better calling for me, and ball wasn't it. I played with some of the greats in the game on every level, and I'm thankful. I traveled, saw the world and made some coin. People ask me all the time about my hoop days. All I say is I wouldn't change it for the world. My path is still going, still unwritten. But I'll tell you this, some of my best experiences and friendships, until this day, come from that little orange ball we call basketball.

Life Beyond the Game: Business, Philanthropy, and Fun

I've branched it out into business, philanthropy, and a lot of different other aspects of my life, not just wealth or entertainment. Entertainment was my bread and meat, how I fed my family and how I made money. But now, since I'm pretty much semi-retired from the entertainment space, I'm doing all that other stuff now with some full-time companies and referring and doing other things.

I don't have a genre that's my favorite. If it's productive, positive, helping, not just making myself profit and being successful at a situation, it has to be something that I believe in, see the potential for growth and is uplifting. And the key is fun. It has to be fun for me to be involved with it. Because I don't look at things I get involved with nowadays as work, because I don't want to work anymore. It just has to be fun. It has to go with the lifestyle and it has to be rewarding on making others successful. That's why I seem to be getting my joy out of doing different things now.

The Bond of Brotherhood: Remembering Marlon

My friend Marlon Edwards and I were born one day apart in the same hospital. Of course we didn't know that we would end up being best friends in our high school days all the way through adulthood until he passed away. But I was born in that same hospital on July 30th, 1973, and he was born there on July 31st, 1973, which means we were in the same incubator room or the same hospital and our parents were in there at the same time. Fifteen years or so later, when we got into high school, we became best friends. Even though he passed, I still have a relationship with his mom and his brother. He's on a mural in my backyard at my house.

Devious (DVS): Building Unity and a Lifelong Legacy

Marlon and I were able to form a brotherhood, a family. He and I were the founders of Devious (abbreviated DVS). He went to school in another part of Rancho Cucamonga. Alta Loma and Etiwanda were rival schools, but we were able to bridge that gap from his school to my school of the basketball players, the hustlers, the playboys, and all those different things. Our organization grew into businessmen, hustlers, and money makers. Now, some of those core members, of course, are businessmen, fathers, and still have the same relationship that we did as kids.

The DVS crew

All of the family and organization we had comes from the DVS family. It was definitely a rarity at that time because you had Crips, you had Bloods, you had a couple Latinos, you had people from different cities, different schools, and we just put a collective group of these guys that, of course, at the time we were kids, but me and Marlon were able to put this together, and like I said, to this day, we still have a great bond.

We have a text chain that we still honor Marlon in. One guy from that organization is my tax guy. Another guy became a successful stunt man. My cousin and I became businessmen. Some great guys came out of there. But I think the face of us uniting as youngsters and staying close and looking out for each other, when there were hard times or homelessness or needed a place to stay or needed something, somewhere to eat, some food or something, our homes and our families connected with all those guys, and some of us turned out okay.

Honoring Much Love: A Legacy of Brotherhood

A lot of the guys in the text chain have tattoos of Marlon's abbreviation for his nickname, Much Love, that we still use to this day. He had a chain with Chinese or Japanese letters that said 'Love.' And his name was Much Love because he spread so much love. Probably 90% of the guys in that group lived at his mom's house at some time or other. They were fed, worked out there, and organized at his house.

Home Going Service of
Marlon Brent Edwards

7-31-1973 ~ 3-1-2004

Marlon's Home Going Service - "MUCH LOVE" DVS Family (circa 2004)

CHAPTER 8
Roots That Run Deep

"Big Percy stands out, not just because of how tall he is, but because he's bright and loud and charismatic and he involves himself in the room. So if you're there, you're going to know who he is automatically. He's the guy who gets everybody up and ready to go.

"His whole energy has always been to get people motivated; with 'let's go get the money, let's make it happen, let's get to the party.' Even when it's time to leave, he'll start telling everybody, 'Hey man, get ready, we're leaving, let's go.'

"When he motivates a young artist, he's got that pitch where they're going to believe it and they're going to get excited and they're going to do what he says. He's a good leader. He has a lot of friends and he knows a lot. He's been around the block and he makes stuff happen. He's a jack-of-all-trades. I'm sure he not only talks the talk, but he proves it too. Once you hear him, then you'll see the results.

"So if you have aspirations to be in it, to be around it, to be on top, those are the kind of people that you need to meet along the way. People who give you direction on how to do it

properly and who don't just sit on the sidelines, cheerleading and watching you make mistakes. He's the kind of person who helps you avoid those mistakes. You definitely learn a lot just by watching him. Learn from him; he's a real OG. He's done it already, so of course you can learn from him. You want to pay attention. For all the years I've known him, he's been a really good friend, like no backstabbing, no betrayal, no shade, none of that stuff. He's been really kind since day one!" ~Too Short

The Guiding Light of My Father

My dad is where I get all my education, book smarts, etiquette, manners and all that stuff. My dad has always been a top educator. The college that I went to and played for is the same college where he was a coach. He was my counselor all through my life. He did this not just for me and my daughter, but also my brother, all my cousins, for a lot of my family members.

Everything dealing with the mentor side, the counseling, making my decisions with school and college and furthering my education, he was that for me. He was that for a lot of family members. But he was that for a lot of inner city kids, athletes, not just me and my family, for a lot of people. And it still shows today how many people that he touched in that capacity. And it's pretty much nowhere in the world that I go and do all my travels that somebody doesn't know my dad. And it even goes to the furthest extent of the Las Vegas Raiders' head football coach. My dad was his coach and counselor.

My dad had influence on my barber, some of my closest friends, even some guys that I didn't even play with, not just their college days, but their life today. A lot of those guys still communicate with my dad when they come into town. They call him, play golf with him, and still get advice from him.

It's different from me being his son and living with him and being around him. At a younger age, you don't want to absorb all that because you just think he's talking crazy to you because he's your father. But now looking back on it and all the people that he's touched and helped, I see the impact that he had on me and others. It's a great thing and I praise him. A lot of people still praise him today.

My dad was a counselor for all. When you go to colleges in California and the United States, before my dad got involved with college sports and counseling, every student (not student athlete) had a normal counselor that went over the classes and different things that you're taking while you're a student, like a guidance counselor.

A Legacy of Mentorship and Advocacy

My dad got into coaching track and football and being involved with so many of these kids' lives. Really, it was more or less when my dad was a top recruiter and seeing talent and kids that just weren't from the area. He saw talent everywhere, so he had to recruit. And a lot of the kids, of course, come out of the ghetto and the urban areas. My dad was able to go in there, get them, talk to the parents, talk to the kids and get them to come to different cities and states to play for him. But it came to a point that my dad wasn't happy and pleased that these athletes were being treated just as athletes and weren't getting the same benefits as any other student.

So my dad came up with the idea and started for all athletes to have counselors. He is the president of all Junior College Academic Advisors for Student Athletes. He started that program and then it carried forward and still exists today. He sits on the board of the NCAA and all types of different stuff my dad has done for the junior college level student athletes. So, yeah, my dad, he's kind of a big wig. He's in the Southern California Sports Hall of Fame. He's in the Mt. SAC Hall of Fame and in the college he played for, Cal Poly Pomona, Hall of Fame. He sits in a prestigious situation for what he's done on the sports and academic sides for student athletes.

A Hall of Fame Educator and Advocate for Student Athletes

Living with my dad, having to hear it and deal with it, me being a great athlete and him seeing the potential in me, not just being a great athlete, a great student, I would get it the worst. Being a stubborn kid, I rebelled against my father and his thinking in certain ways, but I also did take a lot from him that I didn't probably reciprocate at the time. But without my father, I would have probably not gotten a scholarship. I probably wouldn't even have been in school. And I probably wouldn't have continued any of my education and basketball stuff if I didn't have that guidance from him.

Now he is a part of my daughter's life and my daughter's educational path and sports path; they have a great relationship. Of course she's going to rebel just like I did because she's around grandpa a lot. She goes to the school where grandpa's name is on buildings. And grandpa knows, so she can't get away with anything.

Growing Up Under My Father's Watchful Eye

I couldn't get away with anything as well because he knew all my teachers. He knew where I was. He knew damn near every movement I made on campus. So, it was a lot of pressure on me, being my dad's son, which was also a blessing. I got away with stuff and got perks and everything else. But now my daughter is going through the same thing. It's kind of a trip.

Would I change my path? No. Would I change the ups and downs that I went through? No. Would I change my attitude and my outlook and what I put into different situations? One million percent.

Lessons Learned: Sports, Dedication, and Self-Reflection

Sports came easy and natural to me and I didn't put in the extra effort or extra time. I didn't really respect my coaches as much as I could and should have. And that's why I wasn't able to really take off. I took it to all the highest levels you could take it, but I didn't take it to my maximum level because my dedication wasn't there. At that time, everybody thinks they're invincible and the shit will last forever. I would just change some of those things. Would I change what has happened and how I came out? No. But would I change some of my thinking and beliefs and take some things a little more seriously? Of course.

Mentors see something in you for whatever it is, music, sports, education. They see something in you that you don't see in yourself. So you have to look at it that way. It's hard as a kid, as a teenager, as a youngster to think that way. But if you, the person reading this book, can do that and use that as inspiration, I think you'll be fighting an easier battle than I did.

The Power of Mentors: Seeing What You Can't See

Nine times out of ten, if somebody's riding on you, if a coach is on you, telling you this and wants you to come in extra and do this and do that and be a leader and everything else, like I said, they see something in you that you don't see in yourself.

> *People don't spend time on other people unless they see something in them and believe that.*

The people in my life and the people that surround me and the people that I know, those are the people that have made it. Those are the people that are successful. Those are the people that did figure out, "My way, my thinking is not working. These hundreds of people and these other people that are telling me the same shit every day, harping on me about the same shit. It's not just one person. It's a bunch of people telling me the same shit about me. Those are the people that I know in my life that have made it."

And that goes for the Snoop Doggs of the world, to the Matt Barneses, and the Wiz Khalifas to people that I know that I grew up with who are now doctors and lawyers and everything else. They took that advice and said, "What? My way is not working." And it took me a little longer, but I did the same. It took me a little more heartache and a little more ups and downs and trials and tribulations. But it came to a point, in my 20s, that I had to figure it out, but I did. And I'm happy with the result.

The other people that made it to the NBA and got record deals and became successful business owners and everything, they did it a little sooner. And that's why they made it to the "pinnacle" of their career or their profession.

So no matter when somebody changes their attitude, that attitude shift can still be very, very powerful, whether it's early, somewhere midstream or later even. It's life changing. And it goes for every genre of life, every genre of career, every genre of profession. It's not just one particular person that the light switch has to hit. It's for everybody.

I should be a walking testimony of it. Like I said, I was a great athlete. I had things given to me and everybody thought my life was peachy keen, but it wasn't. I had a lot of trials and tribulations and ups and downs that now, looking back on things, I brought them on by myself. Not like I didn't have the opportunity.

Did I squander and fuck up the opportunity? Probably. Did I take advantage of those situations that were laid out for me? Probably didn't. Did I think everything was going to be here forever and last forever and think I was invincible and it couldn't happen to me? Yeah.

It came to a point that I had to wake up and say, "You've got to stop blaming everybody else and blame yourself for the things that are happening to you. It's an easy fix. It's an easy change because you have the potential and the path that's set for you is a great path if you want to go out there and get it."

Turning Point: Embracing Responsibility and Change

And it just came to a point that the way I was living, the things that I was doing, the people that I was hurting, it's not where I wanted to be. And I felt in my inner self and inner being that I was letting a lot of people down and I was letting myself down. I had so much more to give. Once I came to that point, I'm not going to say every day has been great, but I haven't had any bad days. I've been able to come and go as I please. I've been able to walk through a lot of doors that I couldn't have walked through if I didn't make those changes. And being able to walk through some of those doors is the key. If you can't even get your foot in the door, then you're not going to have an opportunity to advance. To be able to walk through a door and say your ideas and sit at the same table with certain people, that's half the battle.

You're running from your responsibilities. You're running from the fear of being great. You're running from all the things that you're capable of doing, but you're scared to succeed and fulfill these dreams and fulfill these things that you have the natural gift of doing. And I was in that mode, kind of like I was sabotaging my own self.

Instead of just looking in the mirror and being like, "What, these people that you're blaming, these are the core people that really genuinely love you and want you to succeed and have been trying to help you. They're not talking down to you. They're talking to you." And I wasn't listening. Those same people, a lot of them, are still in my life and look at me now and are just so happy and pleased. "I knew you had it in you. I knew you could do it." And it's crazy.

Just imagine what I could have done if I listened a little bit earlier. And that goes from family to friends to people more successful than me, younger than me, that have seen my journey, that have seen me now and seen the way that I've grown as a man, a father, a businessman, a mentor. I could have easily not been here.

I'm still going and I still have a lot more to do. And I know I do. Every day I wake up and I know I have some more stuff to do, some more stuff to give, something more. I still have another journey. I'm in the second part of my journey. It's a blessing to wake up and feel that energy and feel that I'm still relevant.

Faith and the Belief in a Higher Power

I definitely believe in God, but my theory on God or Jah or Muslim religion or Jewish or whatever it is, has always been when it comes to religion, *as long as you believe in something that is greater than you*, I don't care if it's a head of lettuce, I don't care what it is, as long as you believe that while you're here on this earth, doing what you're doing, there is something that created you, that has given you the energy and the power to be here and to be great.

Because if you think about it, every day thousands and thousands of people don't wake up. But whatever it is, natural causes, health issues, car accidents, whatever it is, for you to still be here and still moving and still having the energy to breathe, it has to be something greater than you. And that's why I, like I said, don't judge people on religion. I went to a Baptist school as a kid. I got people that are Catholics. I have all types of people, different religions in my family.

I respect all religions. I believe in a lot of the stuff that the Muslims go through. I believe in a lot of different religions. I take bits and pieces from them and incorporate it into my daily living, but I don't judge. I've never judged a person based on their religion, and I've never judged a person based on their culture, because I'm mixed with so many different things. So, yes, I do believe in a higher power. I do believe there is other life, other than just us on Earth. There has to be. Why are *we* just *the* chosen planet? If you think about it, there are other forms of life.

Look at the animals. The animals have been here the longest, so that should tell you. We all come from the origin of animals. We are now just an advanced branch of an animal, and that just has to deal with the things that are out there. There are other solar systems and other planets that we haven't even touched that are out there, and I believe in all that. You have to.

Family Roots and Uncle Milton's House of Love

I've always had family all around me, and I've learned a lot from them. Uncle Milton, my oldest uncle from my mom's side, did two tours in Vietnam. We all call him Uncle Milty. He is the oldest sibling from my grandmother's children. He and my auntie have the same father. He's a military guy, funny guy, different kind of guy, but everybody loves

Uncle Milton. He now lives in Arizona, living his best life, retired, laid back, real chill. The whole city knew Uncle Milton because he had kids. He had five or six kids, and they all did different things.

Uncle Milton: A Pillar of Family and Fun

Uncle Milton's house, in the neighborhood, was kind of like a party house, because he liked to party with my aunties and my other family members, and barbecue and cook, and have domino tournaments, card tournaments, picnics and camp outs in the backyard with the kids and all the family and friends.

Even though my auntie's house was less than five minutes from my grandmother's house, Uncle Milton's house was two minutes from my grandmother's. And it was just another central location that you could always go to if you needed a place to stay, go see your cousins, get something to eat, relax, or ride your bike over there.

We had so many different stops throughout the neighborhood that were real family members, and Uncle Milton's house was kind of like a party house for us kids and adults. He liked to have fun and drink his beer. He was into boxing, so all the big boxing matches I can remember as a kid would be at his house. The good barbecues, and some family functions, and all that stuff. A lot of those were at his house. Great times, great memories, pure love, family first.

CHAPTER 9

Second Chances and True Love

"When I think of Percy, I think of connection. I think of support. I think of someone that will take your call, stop what he's doing, and listen to you. And if there's anything that he can do to support what you're doing, he's going to do it. He's going to give you a real ear. He's going to give you a real answer. If he cannot help you, he'll tell you no. But then he'll say, 'Give me a second, let me see if I can do something else.'

"He's been very impactful in my life as I went and worked in different industries. And then I progressed into ministry and then got my doctorate in divinity. He has been a support system since day one. He's always brought opportunities to me that have allowed me to shine in different places where I would not have normally had the opportunity to shine. He is someone that continuously stays with his ear to the street. He knows what's going on. He knows who is a who's who. And he knows exactly how to maneuver around the industry with all the issues and problems that are in the industry. And he doesn't let anything that could possibly hinder him. He doesn't let it stop him.

"He's the type of person that if somebody builds a wall to stop him, he'll break it down. And then he'll make his

119

own way. And if you don't want to let him in the door, he'll buy the land next to you and build a house and create doors for everybody else and himself to not only get into the door but to defeat you. But he's not somebody that you don't want to give opportunity to because all he'll do is create it. He's a connector, a creator, a supporter. He fights for people. And he stays in his own lane. If it's in his wheelhouse, he'll do it. If it's not in his wheelhouse, he'll simply say, 'That's not in my wheelhouse,' and he'll walk away from it. He does not owe anybody anything. He always makes sure that he keeps his word. And he's somebody that you can always depend on. That's really what I can say about Percy at the end of the day.

"Read this book with an open mind so that you can be in the same mind as Percy because he thinks with an open mind. He's a person that will say something, and you may not understand it. But if you have an open mind, you'll be able to have great perspective and great insight. And you will learn something from him and use the information that you learn to teach somebody else.

"In parting words, I say, "Thank you, Percy, for being a part of my life." I look forward to him always being a part of my life. And I love him to death. I love him like a big brother."
~Dr. Jimmie Magette

Understanding the Importance of Family History

I think it's important for a young person to know their history. If a person knew their family history, starting back from their ancestors to their grandparents to their parents, I think this would help a lot of the younger generation understand the struggles, understand the plight of their family and how they became and how they're here. I've always been intrigued with the history of my family, from my grandmother's side to my dad's side, of knowing where I came from. Going back to just your family part, now you have to take it to the next level and say, 'Well, how did my family come about?' and that comes from something greater than you, because if you go back into the history of your family, everybody came from somewhere. Nobody was dropped where they were.

This is the tribulation of you, me, my kids, my grandmother, and everybody else. That all comes from the belief of knowing there's something greater than you for this world. Once you grasp that and start knowing your history and knowing about whatever you're going to pray to and be thankful for and get the blessings from and everything else, it opens up your values of life. It opens up your horizon on how things are built and how people can live as one and come together.

Once you understand that and understand you're not here by yourself, you can put down all those differences and all those stupid beliefs that are learned... because a lot of the dumb beliefs and everything else are passed on from ignorance. Racism, hatred, all these different things come from learned attributes.

Breaking Free from Learned Ignorance

Ignorance is not in you when you're born. These things have been passed on from generation to generation, and it's that.

I've been super, super blessed to be so diverse in my thinking, diverse in my family, and diverse in the things that I've been able to see and be a part of. That's why my story, I think, needs to be heard, just because it could have easily gone the other way. I just didn't want to be stuck in a box. I didn't want to be like everybody else. I stood out at a young age, not just by my look, but I *was* different. And I felt that at a young age, that me being different was going to be a part of my journey for the rest of my life, and it has been.

Embracing Diversity and Being Different

I teach that to my kids, to my artists, or people that I'm involved with. In any kind of capacity in my life, I teach that being different is a good thing. It's definitely the way I carry myself and live my life.

I'm kind of pulling the 'it' factor out of them like it was pulled out of me. I'm letting them know to stay with it, keep that energy, keep that fire of what you really desire and like and enjoy doing. Because if you have that passion, that real genuine passion for something, it can probably turn into your lifelong job, career, hobby, or passion.

If it's no positive energy, no good flow, nothing that's being beneficial to the group and contributing, I will turn it down. Nowadays, in my second phase of life, even though it could be a lot of fun, or it could be some fast money, or whatever the different situations may be, nine times out of 10 I don't really want to be a part of it. I pull myself out of it all the time. And that has come from my stomach and my gut, my intuition on things. People have said it for a long time, a lot of times, that they think I have some kind of predictive future, and if I say something, then a couple days later the shit happens. I've heard it a lot throughout my life. And now, sitting back looking at it, it is kind of true. Some of the things that I say, and some of the things that I predict, it's crazy that it happens. It's just like somebody making a vision board and putting their thoughts and their goals and their wishes that they can imagine, *feel* it, and *see* it every day.

The Power of Intuition and Manifesting Dreams

I throw a lot of things out into the universe and a lot of times, they come back.

I'm not around my daughter Destiny as much as I want to be, or could be, just because I'm in a different state now. Destiny is an old soul, a destiny baby. I wasn't thinking about having any other kids. I wanted a son and I couldn't find the right person. At that stage in my life, I knew I wasn't going to be settling down with anybody. But I did want to try to make a son; it has always been a dream of mine. And Destiny was the outcome of me trying to make a son. I was happy that I had another healthy child; I was not disappointed.

As Destiny grew, I spent the first two years constantly in her life. It was a nice flow of energy and we bonded. She bonded with my grandmother, with my mom, with a lot of different family members. And that's what I wanted. I knew I had to get back out there working and hustling and traveling the world, the same pattern that I had with my oldest daughter. I needed that instant gratification and that instant bond with my kids because I knew my path and what I had to finish and complete in my life.

Destiny: A Bridge Between Generations

Destiny and I have a great bond. Like I said, I don't spend as much time with her as I should or could, but when I come home, and when I'm back in California, I do make time for her. I call her all the time, even though I'm away.

Destiny is a healer and is very smart. She bridges the gap between a lot of family members, not just on my side, but also on her mother's side. She's the first grandbaby for her grandmother on the other side, so she is spoiled rotten. And she is a real offspring of this new generation of technology, AI, crypto, just all the different things that come from this generation that they're privy to and able to see and experience with all the things that are right at their fingertips.

From a young age, she gravitated to all those different things, and now she's using them in her daily studies and walk of life and how she carries herself, which is kind of different because I didn't grow up that way. We were outside and active and everything, and she's a very active kid, but she's into this technology, and I know she's going to do something great later in life because of her getting involved early with these different things. She'll have a comfort level that maybe older generations won't have as easily. So, Destiny is, like I said, a lover, a healer, and she knows both sides of her family, from the oldest to the youngest. I don't know the path for Destiny right now. I kind of knew my oldest daughter at an early age of being an athlete and having a lot of my different qualities and traits. But Destiny has a lot of my different qualities and traits, so I don't know if she's going to be an athlete.

I had more access to my oldest and didn't have to rely on anybody else to take her anywhere and put her in different activities. Destiny's mom's beliefs are way different than mine. We kind of clash, so I don't get involved because Destiny is with her.

Daddy and Isabella

Daddy and Destiny

Auntie Mildred: The Family Matriarch

Next I'll talk about my Auntie Mildred, my mom's oldest sister. There's an older brother, and then it's my auntie, who is the middle, and then my mom is the youngest. My auntie is the new matriarch of the family after my grandmother passed. Everybody knew that this was going to be her title just because of how she kept the family together and how she dedicated pretty much the second part of her life to taking care of my grandmother. With that, you get a lot of love and a lot of respect from everybody in the family. I don't think, just looking back and thinking, there's anybody in my family that has anything or can say anything bad about Auntie Mildred, just because of the sacrifices that she has done for everybody in our family.

My auntie is a tough cookie. She doesn't let everybody into her world, but she does let everybody in her world, if that makes sense.

Growing up, my auntie was tough. She was stern. She didn't do a lot of yelling, but you just knew her way. You came to her house, you knew how it had to be taken care of. No bullshit, no extras, no drama. And if you kept it that way and kept it respectful, you'd have a good time at her house. And her house, other than my grandmother's house, was second in command. It was where everybody wanted to be because she always cooked. Four or five cousins lived at her house, which was right across from the neighborhood park. Her house was three minutes, at the most, five minutes walking distance to my grandmother's house and two or three minutes walking distance to my uncle's house. The main high school was five minutes walking distance from her house. The main pool, the main community center, five to ten minutes from her house. Her house was the hub, central location, the epicenter of me growing up in the city of Pomona.

You can only do so much at grandma's house, because it's just grandma. There were other kids there and everything else and that's when you went to grandma's. But for all the fun and all the activities and seeing all the other cousins, you always would start off at Auntie Millie's house. That's where you wanted to spend the night.

The Hub of Family: Auntie Millie's House

Even though everybody's older now, if you celebrate holidays and come into town, you're stopping at Auntie Millie's to see her to eat good and fellowship. It was the same house when we were kids.

Now, my Uncle Milton's wife, who was my godmother, and of course my aunt through marriage, she's a part of my life, but my grandmother only has three kids. Later on down the line, I got close to my dad's brothers. They've always been a part of my life, but they lived in the Bay Area, and then the other uncle lived in Minnesota.

They've always been a part of my life. On that side of my family, we became closer later because we all have a love for golf. Throughout the years, the love of golf brought me, my dad, and his brothers a lot closer together.

I have cousins and I'm close with all of them. Of course everybody has a favorite cousin and all that stuff, but I love all my cousins the same. I have better relationships and better communications with some, just like everybody. But my two favorite cousins, one is my cousin Meshon because we're the same age and we're kind of born in the same era, same year. And me being my mom's baby and at the time my cousin Meshon was my auntie's baby, we grew up together, same crib and everything.

Meshon is kind of like me. She takes care of her mother. She's family oriented. She stepped out on her own. She didn't get caught up in the bullshit and carved her own path from going into the army, and working in the correctional facilities and being involved with the criminal justice system. And those, coming out of the urban area and the ghettos and the parts of town, that's kind of frowned upon, getting involved with law enforcement and going into the military services. She didn't waver from it. She did it on her own and became successful at both and took care of her mom and took care of her family via those resources. So I respect her on that, but she and I (and everybody knows it) would always have a battle of being grandma's favorite. We're the same age and we've been a part of grandma's life since we both were born. We were always with grandma and we were the closest to grandma. One, she lived around the corner from grandma, but I think she and I are the people that would visit grandma the most, take her food, spend time with her, call her the most from kids to adulthood. And even at the funeral, other cousins who got up there would say, "Well, I know Damien and Meshon think they're granny's favorite, but I'm granny's favorite." Going up there, joking, but everybody knew that Meshon and I were in competition for being granny's number one.

Grandma's Favorites: A Playful Competition

Even to this day, we talk about it, laugh and joke about being grandma's number one. And I give her the benefit of the doubt. I say, "Okay, I was the number one grandson and you were the number one granddaughter." We had that bond with grandma and I think we did the most for her while she was here.

It wasn't about material things. Even though we did material things, grandma would turn down a lot of stuff, but it would just be the phone calls and visiting. And anytime we were in town or whatever, we would pop in on her.

Cousins Who Became Family Pillars

My cousin Meshon's relationship probably was a lot deeper with grandma because when my cousin went to the military and my aunt moved to Vegas and was doing her own thing, grandma working a full-time job, took care of Meshon's only child, Shonell, while my cousin was in the military. She was an older lady still working and handling her business and taking care of her granddaughter's child. I know that's how their bond strengthened.

Shonell lived with grandma. It was a blessing because her school was 15 feet away from grandma's house, just on the other side of the street. That relationship of being grandma's granddaughter's daughter, they had an amazing bond all the way to the end. Shonell's in her early 30s now.

Then my other favorite cousin comes through marriage. He's been in my life since I was a kid. When his dad married Auntie Millie, John had three kids in Detroit and Auntie Millie helped him get those three kids so they could be with him. They formed their own little 'Brady Bunch.'

I was able to get my favorite cousin through marriage from that relationship. And that's my favorite cousin to this day. We're like brothers. His name is Terrance, but everybody named him Sugar Bear because he looked like the Sugar Bear guy on the box of cereal. He's my favorite cousin. He's probably a year older than me, but that's who I gravitated to. We instantly bonded and it just grew throughout the years.

Sugar Bear: My Cousin and Brother

Sugar Bear owned the Power House Records label that helped me expand into getting my management company and everything else.

And another reason why I kind of gravitated and moved to Vegas is because he lives here, and he ended up running my store when I opened it. Just a great bond.

Like I said, cousins through marriage and that's been over, shit, 40 years, but we're brothers. He's the brother that I always wanted. He was my crimey, my top dog, my homie, and we've done everything under the sun and more, everything imaginable together. I probably talked about him earlier in other stories, but yeah, that's him. Sugar Bear Flowers.

Me and Sugar Bear, then and now

CHAPTER 10

K.B. aka Her

"A lot of people think that Big Percy is a little abrasive and a little harsh. Really, he's a motivator. But more, he's a bull, he's strong, he's a lion, he's a Leo. He's a good friend, he's a good mentor, and he's a good father, a good family man. I've known Percy for about 30 years now, and I've watched the length of what he does almost from the start to the big mogul that he is now. He's a giver. He likes certain types of people around him. If he likes you, and you seem like a loyal, worthy person, he'll give you the world. He'll open doors for you. Percy is a man of many talents. He knows everybody, and everybody knows him best.

"I've been Percy's photographer and media coordinator for about 25 years. And the things that I see him do with other people as far as, let's say Snoop, for instance, watching him rise through the ranks of being as close as he is with Snoop Dogg right now, over the 20-plus years, watching him bring opportunities together, like the groove. If Snoop just said, "Hey, Percy, I want to do a song with Justin Bieber, but I don't have a line on him, do you?" "Oh, yeah, hold on." Next

thing you know, he'll make the call, and he'll have Justin Bieber and Snoop on the phone. That's his reach. He's your guy behind the scenes. "Oh, you need a book made? Oh, yeah, I got somebody. Hold on. Let me call my girl." And, you know, he gets the ball rolling.

"Everywhere we go, across the United States, somebody knows Percy. The people that aren't around him don't know what he does. And they ask, "Hey, what do you do, why are you around this person (the artist they recognize)? It's the persona and charisma that he has. It's the 'make it happen' that he has. He has the key that is needed to make it move. I've seen that constantly throughout the years, and it's an amazing thing to see. Honestly, it's very motivating. To some people it can be intimidating, but to us, it's very uplifting. It lets us know that, okay, we also can rise to those types of situations. If we're put into those situations, those types of roles, we have somebody that we can call that can possibly connect those dots. He's a dot connector.

"The most important thing that he gives them is hope. Hope is everything, especially if you can see it, then you can achieve it. He puts it in your face. He's changed my life."
~Dave Evans

Me with Dave Evans

A High School Love Story

She was my girlfriend coming right out of high school into college. We had a bunch of mutual friends. I guess I bugged her and made her laugh so much that she finally gave me a chance. We dated our first two years of college. When I received my basketball scholarship, we kind of separated. And then when I got up to the university, I was going through some growing pains and getting into a little trouble.

My university asked me, "What would it take for things to make you happier and things to change in your life?" I said, "Well, you've got to get me back with my girlfriend, get her up here."

A Missed Opportunity

They got a hold of her and offered her a scholarship, a job, housing, cars, everything that she needed to come up to the school and get back with me. She turned it down. Yeah, she turned it down. She told them, "It sounds like you guys just want me to come babysit and do all these other things." So she turned it down and we kind of separated throughout the years and broke up.

We kind of remained friends to a certain extent. Like I said, we had a bunch of mutual friends and she was cool with my family and I was cool with hers at the time.

Reconnecting After Decades

Then as time went on, we were bumping into each other at different events and hanging out throughout the years. After connecting on two or three different times throughout the year, she got married. I went my own way. We lost contact, and life just carried on.

About three years ago now, her sister was at my golf tournament and she happened to be talking to my ex's dad and I hadn't talked to him in years. So she put him on the phone. We talked and it was like old times and he said, "Man, you gotta come see me." So we made arrangements. Come to find out, a guy that works for me who is in charge of all my media and stuff, Dave Evans, he and Kristi's brother (rest in peace) were best friends from junior high to high school. So he and I got to talking and everything and he broke it down like this, Dave's best friend happened to be Kristi's older brother, who dated my home girl, Marisol. And Marisol also dated my brother.

The Small World of Pomona

Wow, talk about six degrees of separation! Such a small world, in the city of Pomona.

So after the golf tournament, when I was talking to the dad and I got to talk to the mom, I still hadn't talked to Kristi. When I got back to Vegas and I was going through Facebook, I looked up one of Kristi's good friends that I went to high school with. I wanted to see if they were still friends and they were. Then I found Kristi's profile and I told her to call me. It took her a couple of days, but she called and we talked for about a week every day, hours and hours, just catching up, no expectations or anything, just catching up and getting things off our chests.

To make a long story short, after the golf tournament, Dave was going to see them and he picked me. By that time, we had been broken up for probably 28 years and I hadn't been over at her parents' house in about 25 years.

Old Times Revived

She was there, her mom was there, her dad was there, and it was just like old times. They got to see Dave because they helped raise him and it was just like old times.

Me with Kristi aka HIM N HER - then and now

Kristi married into the Muhammad Ali family. She and her husband separated and he had passed away after. So she had some good memorabilia, different things she wanted to get rid of. As a good gesture, trying to impress her, I guess, I bought about $10,000 worth of memorabilia from her. That was my first time seeing her in years. I guess that put a little good blessing in for me.

After that, we kept the dialogue open, hung out a few times. I think I took her to dinner and a couple of events or something. At the time, she was dating somebody for about four years, a younger guy, about 11 years younger than her. She opened up to me that they weren't on the same page.

A Chance to Reconnect

Her dad kind of gave me some kind of hints about what was going on in that relationship. So I took my shot and made it known what my intentions were. And then we went on separate vacations; I went with a friend and she went with him. When she came back, I guess it was over. He got drunk and did some stuff she wasn't happy with.

But, four years, if you guys ain't married and have kids and all that, what are you doing? She was in that same kind of space.

28 Years Later: Back Together

They broke up, so I took my chance. 28 years later, we are now going on two years that we've been back together.

I don't want to ever get married again just because of the experience that I went through, and I know when you put those titles and rules and expectations on it, that's when things get a little funky. I know she had a hard, different marriage and went through some things and everything else.

But she was always close to my family and still is to this day. She got to spend some time with my grandmother before she passed. And come to find out, my grandmother used to tell Kristi all the time that she used to pray every day that she would come back.

Kristi with Granny (circa 1992)

Family Bonds That Last

She and my mom have always been close, so now they're back as best buddies. I send them on trips and concerts without me. I just send them and they go. She takes her mom and friends and my mom comes with her friends.

They've always been close and that's a great thing for them. Kristi hasn't had any kids, but she instantly bonded with my two. My oldest was happy that I finally found somebody that looked out for me and wasn't trying to take advantage of me. So naturally, both my kids built a great bond with her because she's very nurturing.

She and I, when we were together, raised her nephew like he was ours. He was with us all the time because her brother was going through some things and the mom was going through some things. And then the grandparents eventually raised him like he was theirs. He was a big college football player at USC. And now, kind of ironic, he's into the music business like I am.

Kristi has a great relationship with my kids. Actually, my little daughter calls her her best friend. From the very first time they met, they've been best friends! And my oldest daughter has her own relationship with her and they do things and communicate and see each other without me. So that's definitely a blessing.

It's great for me because she was there when I didn't have anything, she actually helped me get my scholarship, helped me with my schoolwork and keeping me focused when I was at the junior college level. And I'm not going to say we both didn't have anything, but we both were struggling. Our parents were well off and did certain things for us. But she was really there for me when I didn't have anything. So I instantly have a trust and genuine love for her.

HER Role in My Life

We're two years in and I've been able to do some things for her and help her out with different situations and take her places and give her certain things that I wasn't able to do when I was a young kid. So that feels good.

Her family has always been a great motivation to me and many others in the Black community just because of how long they've been together. Her dad is a successful businessman and was also a fire chief. They come from a decent area in California. We used to joke, my friends and I'm sure her friends, that their family was like The Cosby Show because they had it together and they looked at the dad and mom in that light. They had a nice house, nice cars, so we used to treat them or say they were like the Huxtables when we were growing up. Her parents are still together. They still have the same house and still do a lot of different things for people and their family, and people not in their family.

An example of real Black love, real family matters, and real strong values.

Kristi and me (circa 2024)

Conclusion

As I've said, we all come from humble beginnings and poverty-stricken areas, but you don't have to stay there. *There is more for you.* And once you become more productive and more successful than whatever you're doing, the end goal is to get out of that environment and have your family in a better situation. There's opportunity for anybody and everybody.

If you consult me, I will tell you straight up, if your music sucks, I don't sugarcoat shit. If you've got something in you, not on you, and do what I ask of you, you'll make it. A hundred percent, I'll get you there. But if not, you'll know. Then, you can focus on the natural talent that *is* your 'it factor' and you can do well with that. If it's not in my wheelhouse, I'll tell you that too. I don't want to waste your time, and I don't want you wasting mine.

People who've consulted me and gone and done what I suggest, they come back and tell me, "Thanks Unc!" I hear it every day.

I've been blessed, and I'm aware of how different things might have gone for me. I am blessed because I had a lot of family who looked out for me, wanted the best for me and did their best for me. My grandmother, my parents, my auntie, these people have made me. I am extending the same love to my children, to carry forth the legacy of always reaching for better, for them and their family.

Pomona was a great place, and it was also rough. We had to come a little harder, a little tougher. I had a lot of friends from different backgrounds, and so I never saw the differences. I've been colorblind my whole life. Not everybody has had this, but you have to rise above the race thing.

Learn to associate with all backgrounds, colors, races and regions. You never know who's going to be your friend, your business associate, your partner, your family. Rise above it, and you'll be closer to the success you seek.

Learn from your own mistakes and the mistakes of others. The sooner you know to stay out of jail, avoid any kind of trouble, the easier and safer it will be. If you get yourself in jail, it's *hard* to get out. I've been in jail, more than once, but I've been out now for around 30 years or more, and I plan to never go back. If you land yourself in *prison*, it's nearly impossible to get out.

I've hit rock bottom two or three times, but I didn't stay there. I've had flack, I've heard the hate, I've done time. But, a day above ground is still a good day and a day that can advance you.

No matter what your situation is, you can do better. The strong survive, you just have to know that it's worth it, to give it all you've got and look forward to brighter days ahead.

Give a lot of love and a lot of love will find you.

Remember your roots, do what you do for the love of doing it, and keep moving up to better and better opportunities and environments. It's there for you. Rise up and meet it!

~Big Percy

LIL "P

CAPITAL "P"

What's next?

My movie is coming soon.

After that, I'm not sure where life will take me, but I'm open to all the possibilities and opportunities.

Acknowledgments

I want to start out and say a special acknowledgement to my two daughters, Isabella and Destiny. Without them, there's no me, a real, true girl-dad.

Me and my daughters

I want to thank all my family members and friends.

I want to thank all the RMM supporters throughout the years.

I want to thank my junior college which is Mount San Antonio Junior College.

I want to also thank Doggy Style Records, and the entire Dogg Pound family. My DVS brothers.

I want to thank the south side of Pomona, and the entire city of Pomona.

I want to give a shoutout to Lynda Sunshine West and her company, Action Takers Publishing. And we also want to shout out George Lopez and the George Lopez Foundation for linking me up with Lynda Sunshine during George's golf tournament. And then also a shout out to Helena Hope Wall for spending these last few months with me, making my story and my vision come to life.

And last but not least, I want to thank all my haters, haha! Without having any haters, there's nothing for them to hate about.

I want to thank "P" aka me, for "P" on the world, Jah bless, God's work, I'm just a vessel.

FAMILY PICS

153

CELEB PICS – FRIENDS OF RMM

MIX OF PIX

COMPANY LOGOS AND MAJOR
EVENTS AND PROJECTS

RMM BigP

Made in the USA
Las Vegas, NV
20 December 2024

14855956R00098